Praise for
The Mind of the Futurist

The management ideas of CK Prahalad are widely known. This book shows the passion and integrity that drove him and enabled him to turn ideas into impact in the classroom, boardroom and the real world. *The Mind of the Futurist* is more than a tribute; it is a call to action. His boundless optimism and call to focus on the future is more relevant than ever.

Deepa Prahalad

The Mind of the Futurist is far more than an illustration of CK's incredible intellect and wisdom. It reminds us that CK's real genius was provoking brilliance in everyone around him. With this rich compilation of CK's thinking comes a clarion call to carry forward his work and realize the promise of his great vision for India and the world.

Liz Wiseman, WSJ bestselling author

This is a book that celebrates the ideas of a remarkable human being. As an academic and thinker CK Prahalad had few equals. As a man he combined humility with a burning desire to improve the lot of his fellow men and women, especially those afflicted by poverty. His ideas changed the way the world thinks about the people at the bottom of the pyramid and much more besides.

It is testament to his global reputation that he topped the Thinkers50 ranking in 2007 and 2009, the first Indian thinker to do so. Realistic and pragmatic about the challenges facing India, CK was optimistic about the country's future.

"India will take one step forward, half a step backward, a quarter step sideways," he told us the last time we saw him. "It is never going to be a smooth transition and we should not expect it. But directionally, I am extremely positive on where India is going."

CK was a great man – and a great Indian. If ever a country needed his ideas, it is India today.

**Des Dearlove and Stuart Crainer,
Founders of the Thinkers50**

C K Prahalad

The Mind
of the
Futurist

Rare Insights on Life, Leadership & Strategy

Benedict Paramanand

𝓌

westland ltd

61, Silverline Building, 2nd Floor, Alapakkam Main Road, Maduravoyal, Chennai 600 095

No. 38/10 (New No.5), Raghava Nagar, New Timber Yard Layout, Bengaluru 560026

93, 1st Floor, Sham Lal Road, Daryaganj, New Delhi 110 002

First published by westland ltd 2014

ISBN: 978-93-84030-31-5

Typeset: PrePSol Enterprises Pvt. Ltd.

Printed at Thomson Press India Ltd.

To The Jesuit Fathers

Contents

Foreword

The community of practitioners, academics and commentators in the field of management is young in comparison to many other professions. Even when I graduated from college in the mid-1960s, in India, the concept of the professional manager was not widely understood. That is why I did not study at one of the upcoming IIMs, and preferred to go to an IIT. But CK, my senior in age by four years, did study at an IIM (Ahmedabad, for the benefit of IIMA chauvinists!). One of his classmates was Dewan Arun Nanda, who became my colleague at Hindustan Lever, and later acquired distinction as the 'Rediffusion entrepreneur'.

How did CK become a legend even during his lifetime? His physically exhausting travels to India, his relentless hectoring of risk-averse Indian entrepreneurs, his lofty sermons on globalisation, his invitation to managers to play in his innovation sandpit and much more: all these were the stuff of CK's grand calls to action. Ideas like Core Competence and Fortune at the Bottom of the Pyramid are synonyms for CK. That is why he became a legend.

In this book, there is mention of an episode when CK was engaged in deep discussion with a business leader. The discussion strayed into a product domain that was connected with another company where he was a director. CK promptly closed the discussion. That showed his character. I was that business leader. I was hugely impressed by the clean line that he drew, and very elegantly, at that.

CK was an intellectual giant, but he did not wear that attribute on his sleeve. He was approachable and friendly. CK's ideas were scrutinised and studied during his lifetime, but not CK himself. We all thought there is time to do that later. Alas, we were all wrong.

Now Benedict has started the process of remedying that lacuna. He has painstakingly reconstructed an authentic compendium of who CK was, what CK stood for and what made CK so magnetic: **a truly inspiring effort about a truly inspiring thinker.**

The Catholic Church recognises its great leaders through a four-stage process. The process itself begins five years after the person has died. The first stage is Servants of God, then Venerable, then Blessed, and finally after an exhaustive parsing of accumulated evidence, Saint (beatification or canonisation). The management world has no such rigorous process. But, for sure, the Servant of Management process is on. Benedict has made an interesting and fascinating contribution.

R. Gopalakrishnan
Director, Tata Sons Limited
Mumbai, 1 June 2014

Foreword

I knew CK Prahalad since he was a graduate student at IIM-Ahmedabad and then at Harvard Business School. We continued our friendship over time and became a bit closer when he became active with TiE (The Indus Entrepreneurs), moved to San Diego and became an entrepreneur.

I was in utter shock and disbelief when I learned that he passed away in San Diego in April 2010. He was too young and had so much more to contribute to the management and strategy disciplines. Fortunately, his legacy is eternal and he will be always remembered in the same way as we continue to remember Peter Drucker through his writings.

Just as we rediscover and admire great poets, playwrights and authors, I am convinced that CK Prahalad will be rediscovered and admired further in the future by both management professionals and academic scholars.

CK was not only a brilliant thinker but an equally a great writer. He articulated and persuasively advocated his perspectives and frameworks which often either challenged the prevailing dogma or expanded the thought horizon. **Like Peter Drucker, CK was the bridge between the academic world and the real world**. He carried unique solutions to urgent problems of companies and industries. His long term influence on Philips in the Netherlands is legendary. At a young age, he agreed to join the MAC (Management Analysis Center) group founded by two Harvard professors and had great consulting practice.

He also brought to the academic world many ideas and practices of the real world. This was not only through great articles in Harvard Business Review (HBR) but several classic books including *Competing For The Future* (with Gary Hamel); *The Fortune At The Bottom Of The Pyramid;* and *The Future Of Competition* (with Venkat Ramaswamy).

CK is well known for three key concepts. First is the discovery of a company's core competence and using it not only as a competitive advantage, but also for diversification. Second, he saw the future of competition as the advantage arising from pooling core competencies between the suppliers and their customers. This led to the co-creation of value as a key concept. And of course, he became even more widely known in the public policy and economic development circles from his writings on uplifting the Bottom of the Pyramid (BOP) consumers and markets.

While we all miss him, we will also remember him forever.

Jagdish N. Sheth
Charles H. Kellstadt Professor of Business
Emory University (U.S.A)

Introduction

Every child has heard of the 'five blind men and an elephant' story. If you ask them about the moral of the story, chances are you will hear many or you will hear none. It's not their fault. When there are many versions of the same story, its interpretations too are likely to be varied. Rumi, the 13th century Persian poet and teacher used the story to tell his students about the limits of individual perception. The most imaginative interpretation, it appears, is how one part of an elephant can be imagined to be greater than the whole.

Could late Prof. CK Prahalad be the proverbial elephant in the story? His students swear they didn't know a better teacher; CEOs say no one mentored and coached them like he did; economists say no one redefined the consumer and poverty as radically as he did; his colleagues say they learnt from him how to look at the big picture; his peers say everything he did was contrarian. It's apparent that CK's body or work was so vast that even his daughter Deepa Prahalad says: *"Even we sometimes struggle to understand how much he really did."*

How was it possible then for a man to be so profoundly influential in every field he worked in during his 35-year career? How did he align everything he did to a larger cause and tango effortlessly at their cross section? And, what was that cause?

This book is my invitation to experience the late CK Prahalad's panoramic life in full splendour through a combination of fascinating anecdotes and insightful experiences.

I was inspired, you could even say, provoked to write this book when I heard several Indian CEOs speak about how CK inspired them at a memorial lecture his alma mater, Loyola College, had organized in Chennai in 2011, a year after CK had passed away in April 2010. The questions that zipped through my mind were – *How much of CK's significant impact on Indian business is known outside CEO circles? Why should all the credit for India's dramatic business and economic turnaround be hogged by a few politicians and a handful of daring business leaders? Why aren't business coaches, mentors and thought leaders celebrated for their contribution outside the precincts of business associations? And why can't a history of Indian business after 1991 be written with CK as the central figure when he is the common factor seamlessly connecting many Indian business leaders?*

I was lucky to start with Anand Mahindra, Vice Chairman of Mahindra & Mahindra and one of the most articulate business leaders I've met. A Harvard graduate, he loves using sports lingo to make a point. When I asked him plainly what he thought about the role business coaches played in India's business resurgence, he shot a straight volley: *"Football teams, like businesses, don't win only because of the strategy or the equipment they wear or because of the size and girth of their leaders; they also win because of their coaches giving them courage, direction and the inspiration to go out onto the field in the first place. I think we don't give enough credit to fuzzy things; the abstract contribution of our business coaches."*

CK was more than just a business coach. You will see later in the book from the personal anecdotes of leading global and Indian business leaders like Ratan Tata, Adi Godrej, Paul Polman of Unilever and Bill Nuti of NCR Corp how CK played a pivotal role in fundamentally transforming their mindsets and enriched their global outlook which had a far-reaching impact on their businesses over a period of two decades.

Ram Charan, CK's contemporary and a highly respected global management guru says: *"CK got business leaders to think in a broader scope, got them to think long term, got them to think in a global context. This is a huge contribution."*

This book is essentially a chronicle of how CK, an Indian-born American management professor profoundly impacted and deeply influenced a sizable number of global and Indian entrepreneurs, business leaders and senior executives from 1980 to 2010 — a period in which most ideas, rules, systems, people management practices and leadership styles for running a business were rewritten. It was a period when the world order changed dramatically as economic power and business growth gradually shifted from the West to the East. The purpose of business too started to shift from only profit to include people and the planet.

Readers can see how CK shaped the evolution of this new order in the 'Global Impact' chapter though his articles, books, teaching, consulting and being on the boards of large multinational companies. The anecdote on CK's role in the revival of Philips is riveting.

It is no coincidence that the leaders CK worked closely with, who spoke to me candidly, are also the architects of the new order. It includes fascinating cases of how CK's magnum opus – 'Fortune at the Bottom of the Pyramid' (BoP) -- fired the imagination of CEOs and opened up possibilities of creating wholly new products and markets.

Gary Hamel, CK's co-author in several of his seminal works, says that billions of poor people in the world would be indebted to CK as he has completely changed the way business looked at them -- from being seen as a burden to society to being seen as individuals and as demanding consumers. This mindset change has started to have significant impact on the livelihoods of the poor around the world and has opened up new business opportunities.

For businesses, BoP in different forms is driving innovation and growth. Interestingly, you will see how the next phase of BoP is not Fortune AT the BoP but Fortune WITH BoP. When business executives implement this, they are bound to look at their customers as real people, not merely as numbers that add to their bottom line.

Sustainability and how it will drive future business innovation was CK's last big project which he launched with great enthusiasm in 2008. The stiff agenda he has set will guide a lot of businesses that see this as the next big opportunity.

The first three chapters in the book are all about the unbridled spirit of a boy who did his schooling in a vernacular medium school in a small town called Coimbatore and later went on to sit on the boards of the world's biggest corporations. Generous anecdotes help capture CK's vivid experiences as a student; the invaluable lessons he learnt on the shop floor as a young executive with Union Carbide and India Pistons; as a passionate teacher at the Indian Institute of Management, Ahmedabad and at the University of Michigan, who captivated his students to go on to do what was right, not what pays; as an academic who thought his life would be useful if he focussed on the big picture; as a prolific author who, using deep contrarian intelligence, turned many ideas on their head and with his incisive writing style cut through the clutter with razor sharp logic and wit.

Locker Rooms to Trophy Rooms

The heart of the book is in the chapter that discusses CK's impact on CEOs. This chapter – *'Indian CEOs – Turning Sheep into Tigers'* takes the reader on a roller-coaster ride from CK's first annual CEO Forum in Bangalore in 1994 at ITC Windsor Manor to his last CEO Forum at Taj Mahal Palace Hotel in Mumbai in 2009. It captures what transpired during those years and how they were like India Inc.'s, to use Anand Mahindra's phrase, *locker rooms* where CK reprimanded, inspired and led hundreds of Indian business leaders to dream big and act big. The results are there for all to see.

Interestingly, the trigger for CK's 'Transform Indian Business Mission' was a seemingly innocuous incident in Delhi in 1989. When CK asked a group he was addressing if they believed India had the potential to become a global economic power by 2000, only one hand went up. It was the hand of the German ambassador to India. CK felt terribly embarrassed to see not even a half effort by an Indian.

The same night, in his hotel room, CK wrote in his diary; *"How can India get to be in a unique league of nations with US, Europe, Japan, China for creating a new world economic order ?"* CK later said: *"I am happy I wrote it down. That's when I realized we can be there. However, what we do in the next 10-15 years will critically determine whether we belong to the exclusive club or not."* He said: *"In 1817, India accounted for 30 percent of global trade. We have been there before, and we just tend to forget that we did it before."*

The two decades following the historic 1991 economic reforms has arguably been the most dramatic period in India's modern business and economic history – an incredible turnaround from a disgraceful underdeveloped nation status dependent on international aid to that of a potential economic superpower with a table in G-20 summits. CK may well be the key architect of this transformation of Indian business from protection-seeking outfits, terrified of global competition, to respected global players.

He saw India's potential long before many people did and the key role business could play in it. Slowly but surely, CK got Indian businesses to believe in going beyond their profit numbers and contributing to India's transformation and that it was good for them in the long term.

CK believed his mission for India extended beyond reforming its corporate sector. He tried to wean India away from a fixation with the Chinese model of manufacturing. He worked with Arun Maira, Member, Planning Commission and Jamshyd Godrej to relentlessly convey to entrepreneurs that they should focus on their aspirations and dreams and less on their constraints. He made Indians believe that they should focus on the high end, on scope rather than on scale. He argued that India could become the world's manufacturing hub in products that involved knowledge, software and cutting edge research using its vast talent pool.

CK was India's go-to man on the global scene, avidly connecting Indian companies to global corporations, and connecting global corporations to business opportunities in emerging markets. In his no-nonsense style, CK told business leaders that they could aspire to become global only if they raised their quality, governance and business ethics to the highest standards.

By 2003, India Inc. had shed its languid outlook and was ready to look in the eye of the best multinationals. By 2010, many Indian businesses were on par with, and a few even exceeded global standards. It wouldn't have been this smooth if they had not listened to and acted on one of CK's most powerful doctrines – ***Don't follow best practices, instead go on and create the Next Practice.*** In the light of this statement, it's interesting to see how India emerged as one of the top innovation hubs of the world.

Dwijendra Tripathi, the first Dean of the Indian Institute of Management, Ahmedabad, and one of India's most respected business historians says: *"There is no doubt that CK caught the attention of the Indian corporate world such as no management guru has done."*

Ratan Tata, former Chairman of Tata Sons, whose tenure coincided with that of CK's 'Transform Indian Business Mission', concurs: *"While most management gurus asked everyone to think out of the box and then tried to fit them into theirs, CK helped business leaders build their own box."*

The chapter 'Indian IT – The Value Driver' is my attempt at discovering and amplifying a lesser known facet of CK's key contribution to the blossoming of India's information technology sector. The top five IT companies and several Silicon Valley entrepreneurs, who came back to India, had CK's counsel right from the early 1990s. They make up for a majority of the software industry's $90 billion annual revenue.

The chapter titled 'Distilling CK's Writings' by Prof. Manikutty, a retired professor from IIM Ahmedabad, offers a succinct analysis of all of CK's breakthrough ideas from his books and articles. It is a treat for students, teachers and anyone interested in learning how CK's ideas gave organizations a new map to work with.

Indians are Ready to be Led Again

Pride in the idea of India as a nation was dear to CK and he would politely dismiss those who didn't share his belief. Unlike most successful India-born Americans who look at India either condescendingly or as a basket case, the possibility of India sharing the high table with the top five nations in his life time galvanized CK immensely.

CK was inspired by Mahatma Gandhi when he thought about how to serve the poor; he was driven by Jawaharlal Nehru's vision for rebuilding India and fired up by Swami Vivekananda's attempt at awakening India's spirit through economic and moral liberation. CK drew huge inspiration from all these three great Indian leaders during his youth and for charting his India@75 vision and strategy to transform India from a mostly poor, emerging economy to a developed country by 2022. K V Kamath, Chairman of ICICI Bank says: *"Whenever the word 'emerging' is dropped (before India), credit for that should go to CK."*

There's no doubt that CK had a revolutionary's instincts and beliefs. He declared that political freedom meant nothing for Indians without economic freedom. At several keynote addresses, he made the point that *"Indians have won purna swaraj, it is time to fight for purna azaadi,"* meaning, Indians won only political independence in 1947 but are yet to have economic freedom. He called entrepreneurs India's new freedom fighters and believed that only they could minimize the curse of abject poverty. CK famously said that **Indians may be poor, but they are not backward.** This rare insight drove CK to dedicate two decades of his life to India's renaissance.

CK strongly believed that India's biggest strength in the global arena was its ability to play the moral leadership role. While this role may have been dented a bit in recent years, he believed India had what it takes to lead because of its enviable success in running the world's largest democracy and building a vibrant economy, the envy of most developing countries. He said: *"India is a country where universality and inclusiveness are widely practised. We have one of the best advantages very few countries have, including China. Just the sheer diversity of religion, language, practices and ethnicity ... and if we can learn to live in peace, if we can accommodate each other, then we can build a model for the world on how to cope with diversity. That is our opportunity, and if we miss this, then we will be no different from anybody else."*

When CK was asked to keynote at India's 60th Independence Day celebrations in New York City by Confederation of Indian Industry (CII) mentor Tarun Das in 2007, he turned around and said it was no fun talking about what we have already done or not done. It was time to talk about what we can do in the future. His paper titled 'India@75' has been published verbatim in this book as the last and final chapter so that its powerful message and framework inspire readers and policy makers. CII has since set up a strong 'India@75 Initiative' and is working closely with the government in implementing many elements in CK's framework, especially his pet project of training 500 million Indians by 2022 in useful skills.

If CK were alive today in 2014, he would have had mixed feelings about what India has done since he wrote his diary entry in 1989. He would have been very proud to see Indian business houses emerge as respected global players and India figure in the global influential group of nations. But CK would have been appalled at the way India's political economy is being managed and how opportunities have been squandered primarily due to abysmal governance standards.

At a time when India is fighting its own demons, CK's strong recommendations could be handy. In his last and biting speech -- the Nani Palkhivala Memorial Lecture in January 2010 in Mumbai – he said: *"We need to deal with corruption head on. If you don't, you cannot have a widespread entrepreneurial culture. **Corruption must be treated as treason against the nation**. We must focus on individual rights -- not group rights, principles -- not rituals. We confuse rituals with principles, and focus on results, not goals."*

But his bigger concern was India's crisis of leadership that seems to have worsened in recent years. He said: *"The crisis in India is a crisis of leadership. There is no one who is willing to articulate a view of India and Indianness with clarity and force so that the country can come together and make the sacrifices needed to build a new India that the framers of the Constitution imagined. **Indians are ready to be led again.**"*

Those who knew CK personally believe he couldn't have achieved what he has in his life but for his genuine humility, natural flair for connecting comfortably with people at all levels and questioning all assumptions. These traits acted as the source springs from where his intellectual juices flowed. Tata Steel's B Muthuram captures it nicely. *"After every session with him, you come away with a lot of confidence, a lot of faith in yourself, a lot of energy. This has an indirect effect on your organization. He was not elitist. He didn't talk you down. He is someone who puts you at ease and you soon start talking to him as his equal."*

This book is not a biography. In biographies, there is a certain beginning and a definite end. The learning and takeaways from CK's life are eternal. For some, this book could seem like fiction, especially when one looks at the vast ground that is covered here.

For me, this book is a celebration of CK as a person whose life was anchored on the philosophy of doing well by doing good; is a peek into his life's work which made him a legend among management thinkers even when he was alive. But the essence of this book is about how he strived relentlessly, like a man possessed, to build a modern India that could take pride in what it did.

CK's death at 68, in April 2010, came as a shock because he didn't show signs of laxity in his energy levels even though he was ill for a few months. Even during his last days, he kept himself busy dictating a column to his daughter Deepa for *Harvard Business Review* and mailing his friends enquiring about their projects.

Sanjay Reddy, CK's student and Vice Chairman of the GVK Group, is poignant when he says: *"The fire that CK left continues to burn in each of us."* I hope this book ignites the spirit of many more.

"I want freedom for the full expression of my personality."
Gandhi

Chapter One

The Man Behind
the Guru

Let the world judge you for who you are. You have to make things happen on your terms. **CK Prahalad**

If you give 100 percent to everything probably you will enjoy 200 percent of the benefits. **CK Prahalad**

You don't become great at anything by being balanced. To be excellent you have to be completely dedicated to whatever you are doing. **CK Prahalad**

You can break rules but don't break obligations. **CK Prahalad**

The world respects accomplishment. If you don't do what you are supposed to do don't expect respect from what's been done by your ancestors. **CK Prahalad**

On a hot summer day in 1948, a six year old boy and his brother, older by 18 months, ambled through their new convent school corridor to the head mistress's office. Pleased with the boys' spirited 'good morning' she gave a chocolate candy to the fair and handsome senior boy. The not-so-fair, short lad waited for his turn. He kept waiting as she turned to attend to another student.

Distraught, the junior ran to his sister's class and sat next to her. Determined not to attract undue attention, the boy decided to look busy. He took out a pencil and a notebook from his bag and started copying the algebra equations written on the black board. The class teacher didn't mind him being there. After a while, out of curiosity, she walked up to see what the kid was up to. She was stunned to see that the boy had copied the equations more neatly and accurately than many students in the class. The boy was anxiously waiting for the bell to ring. The second it did, he sprinted home to his dad. What transpired at home that evening gives us a glimpse into this boy's mind and how he would grow up to become a man obsessed with fairness and its implications in work places and on society.

CK Prahalad, ninth of eleven children, told his dad, a judge and a Sanskrit scholar in Coimbatore, that he was not going back to that school. After confirming that the incident had indeed taken place from his brother and sister and sensing the boy's deep hurt, his father decided to pull out both the boys from the school. This was a very bold decision, because, in India, convent education has been a safe route to good colleges and jobs. Instead, the boys were admitted to a government-run Tamil medium school, the only other school in the village.
This incident showed how much CK hated unfairness even when he was a child. Until his death, fairness was one of CK's touchstones of life. He not only believed strongly in it, he wouldn't hesitate to demonstrate it at every opportunity. CK studied in this school till the 9th grade and moved to a Corporation school in Madras (now Chennai) before joining Loyola College, in the same city for his degree in Physics.

Most child psychologists believe that childhood experiences shape the personality of people. This episode could well have shaped CK's. Studying in the Tamil medium school alongside very poor students gave

CK a glimpse of the real India. Once, while playing in the playground, he saw a boy run to pick up a fish a kite had dropped. It seemed like the fish was too big for the kite to handle as they seldom let go of their prey. The boy ran home to give it to his mother. This incident made CK reflect on how fortunate he was. He often narrated this incident to his two children, Murali Prahalad and Deepa Prahalad and asked them to see the moral in it – that no one should take their comforts for granted. Studying and playing in a government school with very poor students for nine years influenced how CK connected with the poor. He hated the way the middle class and the rich saw the poor as the dregs of society and that they could survive only through charity. **He was convinced right from his younger days that the only difference between the poor and others was lack of opportunity and not intelligence or physical ability.**

It's clear that the seeds of CK's path-breaking philosophy on how poor countries should fight poverty germinated here. The making of the classic '*Fortune at the Bottom of the Pyramid–Eradicating Poverty Through Profits*' may well have begun in his school days.

People Ahead of Systems

CK was fascinated with Physics and spent most of his holidays in the labs to get a head start with the next year's syllabus at Loyola College. He was keen on pursuing a doctorate in Physics after graduation. Destiny had something else in store for him. CK got a call from Father Lawrence Sundaram, his college principal and a Jesuit priest that Union Carbide, an American chemicals and fertilizer company, was looking for two interns. Union Carbide India Limited (UCIL), now owned by Dow Chemicals, manufactured pesticides and marine products across several locations in India. It enjoyed a good reputation until the horrific Bhopal gas tragedy, one of world's worst industrial disasters killing thousands of people around Bhopal on December 3, 1984.

What started as an internship programme turned into a full-time job for the 18-year-old graduate. CK seemed to enjoy the challenge and the opportunity. It was hard work and he didn't mind it. It required leaving for work at 4.30 in the morning. But in no time, CK faced up to the reality of factory life. He saw that the factory had low productivity and the highly unionized workforce was not motivated enough. Early in his career, CK realized he didn't fit into the system, yet, he didn't want to give it up easily. Firstly, he insisted on working on the shop floor for a week to understand the real issues of the employees. By doing this, he also gained the trust of the workers. Having won the first battle, CK quietly suggested productivity improvements.

It wasn't as easy as CK thought. The workers told him that he was stupid to make an already over-worked workforce work more. CK insisted that they could do much better. When they didn't show any enthusiasm, he challenged them to a contest. The contest was - he would work with them for a week and that his productivity would be better than that of the best worker. If he failed, he would accept their current numbers and would not bother them anymore. It turned out that CK performed much better and the workers had no choice but to accept his new productivity targets.

CK's take away from this episode was – *'You have to have the humility to go down to the lowest level and not be condescending. Until you actually experience what someone goes through, you should not judge them.'* The workers realized that CK wasn't the typical elitist kid who was trying to impress the management. He not only won the contest, he also won their trust. Senior executives were amazed at how a rookie could pull off such a coup.

CK impressed the bosses so much that he was picked to be part of the team to set up a battery plant in Calcutta (now Kolkata), to meet the urgent needs of the Indian Army during the Indo-China war in 1962. The war had already started and India didn't look like it had any chance.

It turned out that putting up a battery plant was the easier part; dealing with workers affiliated to Communist parties was tougher. CK was seen as a rank outsider in Bengal. Because of time pressure, CK had to use the patriotism card to inspire workers. It worked and the Calcutta plant was up and running, producing high quality battle-ready batteries. This experience taught CK that managers could succeed if they made workers feel that they too were part of a mission.

"Underneath it all is the same theme I was looking for when I was 19 years old: how to integrate the patterns of work with human motivation and excellence," CK said in an interview published in *strategy + business (August 9, 2010).*

After the war ended, Union Carbide bosses from the US came to see if the plant was any good since it had been put up in a tearing hurry by Indians. They were stunned to find that a few specifications of the battery plant were far superior to theirs and when they got back, they actually copied a few. A senior executive of the company even asked CK which university in the United States he had got his degree from. When CK told him that he had not stepped outside his country yet and that he was just a graduate from an Indian college, he found it hard to believe.

The Indian Army's appalling defeat by the Chinese broke CK's heart. He was hurt more because India hadn't understood the strategic intent of the Chinese. He was sure that if India had made an effort to know what the Chinese were really up to, India would have prepared itself better. CK would refer to this in many of his talks and showed how India had responded very well when it perceived threats better. India's success in building and launching satellites and building its own super computer in the 1990s when the US denied critical components and technology, were his favourite examples.

CK had spent four years with Union Carbide, yet the company said it could not promote him because he did not have a professional degree. This in a way suited him. Just then, in 1964, the Government of India had started the first Indian Institute of Management (IIM) in Ahmedabad, Gujarat. CK had to face difficult questions from his family and friends as Management was then a very new subject in India. No one had a clue as to what kind of a job one would qualify for after doing a course in Management. Yet, CK took the plunge. He was in the first batch and its first gold medallist as well. Even though an MBA opened the door for a management role in Union Carbide, CK chose to move on. He went back to his favourite city, Chennai to be close to the family since his father had passed away while he was completing his MBA. It helped when he also got a job with India Pistons, a mid-size family-run auto component manufacturing outfit owned by the Amalgamations Group.

While at Ahmedabad doing his MBA, CK would travel around Gujarat to observe the hustle and bustle of life. The difference in approach to profession, education, entrepreneurship and a lot more between Gujaratis and South Indians fascinated him. He found Gujaratis to be action and result oriented while South Indians were keen on earning degrees. This contrast exists even now – Gujarat has more entrepreneurs per thousand than all Indians put together. CK would see people distribute milk in the morning and hold a full time job during the day. Exposure to Gujarat helped ignite CK's entrepreneurial spirit.

A Tale of Two Bosses

Good bosses are those who build and lead high performance teams but a few also choose to play the role of mentors especially if they spot a bright talent. Two of CK's bosses may well have been responsible for CK's lofty aspirations and his discovery of his passion for Management teaching and consulting. CK's first boss at Union Carbide, Divakaran, was a Harvard MBA and a Baker Scholar, the top academic honour at Harvard Business School. He was CK's boss when the new battery plant was built in Calcutta.

Divakaran liked CK's earnestness and problem-solving approach. Although CK was not an extrovert, he showed enough keenness to learn and experiment. The boss first wanted to test CK out. He gave him some of his management books to read with the caveat that he had to come back and tell him how its ideas could be applied in the company and in the Indian context. CK liked this challenge. He was sure his boss wanted to inculcate in him the habit of thinking independently. This could well have been CK's first serious initiation into management thinking. Joining IIM seemed like a natural choice thereafter.

CK found that Industrial Engineering in India in the 1960s had turned into a problem-solving discipline where the unit of analysis was only work, and people played a secondary role. He believed that only by shifting the unit of analysis to people could organizations hope to do well. The first book on Management CK read was *The Human Side of Enterprise* by Douglas McGregor [McGraw-Hill, 1960]. It sparked his interest in the general question – What motivates people? He reflected on how he could apply this concept in the plant where he managed 60 people mostly belonging to Communist labour unions.

He told the interviewer of the magazine *strategy+business*: *"I was already fascinated by the way work and people are interrelated. I knew how to conduct time and motion studies and break work down into its constituent parts. I was reasonably good at it. But I saw that when we broke down the work, it changed interactions among people — and more importantly, the skill levels that were required of individuals. This forced me to stop looking at a company or a factory as the unit of analysis, as industrial engineers did. Instead, I started looking at people and teams."*

This was three decades ago when the 4Ps stood for products, price, positioning and place. Only in the early decade of 2000 another P was added and it meant People. Today, the debate has moved on to whether the customers or the people come first in an organization. The scale seems to be marginally tilting towards people.

MK Raju was CK's second boss and had a bigger influence on him. It was almost like his first boss Divakaran handing over his junior to his successor. MK Raju, Managing Director of India Pistons, was one of the pioneers of the Indian management movement for more than three decades. He was a staunch crusader for liberal economic policies even when subsidies, protection and controls on imports were the usual demands from Indian business leaders. An MS in Engineering from the University of Michigan in the 1940s, MK Raju worked with Ford Motors in Mumbai before joining India Pistons in Chennai. If Union Carbide is where CK cut his teeth, it was in India Pistons that he metamorphosed into an independent minded professional.

CK got to see glimpses of advocacy of a global outlook from MK Raju even when the buzz was for protectionism and subsidies. MK Raju's famous line was - *"I consider it worth being killed rather than ask for tariff protection on a permanent basis. If industry has to grow, it has to face global competition."* This was more than 20 years before India started opening up its economy for competition.

Being with MK Raju, who was very active in the Madras Management Association (MMA) helped CK to interact with many business leaders in Chennai. He even had CK do some research on the management profiles of Indian companies, which SL Rao, a prominent author, bureaucrat and a thought leader on Management, remembers as *"an important contribution."*

CK kept in touch with MK Raju even after settling down in the US as a full time professor and a business consultant. They co-authored a report in 1980 titled *'The Emerging Multinationals: Indian Enterprise in the ASEAN Region'* published by MK Raju Consultants. The report was a candid assessment of why Indian joint ventures in Malaysia were largely unprofitable and offered suggestions to revive them. A chapter titled *'Internationalizing Indian Business – Missing Link'* was critical of the Government of India and business leaders' short-term orientation and inadequate attention to strategy. This study may well have been the beginning of CK's immersion into transforming Indian businesses into vibrant entities. It's also possible that a lot of MK Raju's fearlessness and standing up for what he thought was right rubbed off on CK.

Chennai to Boston

CK discovered his love for teaching in Chennai somewhat accidentally. The India Pistons' job left him with enough time in the evenings to pursue his interests. Chennai seemed thirsty for management ideas especially if it came with practical experience. The Indian Institute of Technology, Madras, offered CK his first break. He taught there in the evenings during week days and on Saturdays, he ran computer simulation games on production planning with two others at the All India Management Association (AIMA) office. CK also worked occasionally on some weekends at the Christian Medical College and Hospital, Vellore, a major facility close to Chennai, scheduling outpatients using operations research tools and technology management. His case study on the hospital for IIM Ahmedabad is regarded as India's first professionally written business case study with wide impact on healthcare management.

Four years in India Pistons and CK was restless. He liked his job but it wasn't giving him the adrenaline rush anymore. CK didn't want to be an industrial engineer all his life. He realized that his heart was in teaching and Chennai did not even have a business school then. He aspired to go where his bosses had been – to the very best educational institutions in the US.

For Gayatri, arriving in Boston in 1972 with two small kids meant a full time job of taking care of them. But CK had different plans for her. A year or so after the family started to settle down, CK insisted that Gayatri too apply for her Master's in Education at the Harvard School of Education.

It didn't sound feasible to Gayatri. Gayatri recollects: *"He said it's time to do your Masters. We had no money at that time, we had two young kids and I said how are we going to manage? He said money is a resource, it's not a constraint, he said they are babies today they will grow up to-morrow, if you don't take this opportunity now it's not going to come back again. He insisted that it should be from Harvard."* Both the husband and wife graduating at the same time at Harvard was something of a record then.

How Gayatri managed to do this baffles her children even now. CK meanwhile enrolled himself into the doctorate programme at Harvard. CK realized how a highly engaged work experience in dynamic conditions helped him relate to complex management ideas and concepts, especially the lively interplay between people and systems. He created a record of sorts at Harvard Business School by completing his doctorate in two-and-a-half-years. When everyone was going gaga over it, CK wondered what the fuss was all about. CK's thesis advisor noted that at 28, CK saw his career path as an opportunity to make an impact. When impact becomes the driving force, usually, a lot of less useful and time-consuming stuff, and even people, find a way of getting out of your way. Soon after graduation, the family headed back to India. CK had turned down job offers and a teaching position at Harvard and other places. Colleagues and friends in the US urged CK and Gayatri to delay their return, as Emergency had been clamped in India, but CK refused to do so.

He began to teach at his alma mater IIM Ahmedabad as he thought that it was the best place to begin his 'Impact India' mission. Although CK enjoyed teaching immensely, he soon grew frustrated with the bureaucracy of 1970s India. He could accept the financial sacrifices involved with coming back, but not the idea that he was not making an impact. After painful deliberation, he decided that going back to the US was his best option.

A window of opportunity opened up when CK heard about a Professor in Ross Business School in Michigan University who was going on a sabbatical. This was a temporary position, yet, CK was willing to take the risk even if that meant moving bag and baggage with his family to Ann Arbor. When asked how he could do such a thing, CK said he didn't believe in waiting for opportunities to show up well-dressed. He had a knack of spotting them early on. His common line to entrepreneurs and students was how opportunities have a way of showing up in funny ways and it was up to them to seize it and make the most of it. **Ideal opportunity is a rare thing and people get old waiting for it.**

CK forced the decision to move to Michigan on himself and his family looking at the volatile political and economic situation in India in 1977. Prime Minister Indira Gandhi's Congress government had declared emergency in June 1975. India was on the boil with many political leaders were sent to jail without trial. Freedom of speech was curbed. Murali recollects: *"Michigan offered at a time when we needed the most. Emergency was no fun for anybody, let's not pretend. We went through some very tense times."*

Values over Expediency

CK was an intense person. It showed on him. Yet, his family says, he was not prone to short-temper. He hated loose talk but enjoyed good humour. Dressing appropriately was very important to him since it showed how much one was serious about a task. Intensity comes naturally to people who are highly goal-focussed and set to achieve their goals through a very high standard of integrity and meticulousness.

Gayatri thinks CK's father was his number one influence. *"We always heard stories about conduct, not about money. CK remembered his father's dedication to learning. He also grew up at a time where there were a lot of restrictions, but nobody was judged based on their background."*

Whether it was in his personal life or professional life CK set his goals – where he would want to be 20 years from now. He would then put five-year milestones on how to get to that goal. 'Fold your future in' is one of his most remembered lines by students and CEOs.

CK admitted he was a workaholic and yet, his friends and family say, he was a complete family man. Gayatri says: *"We were never members of any club. When he came home, his house was his palace. The most relaxing thing for him was to go for a long walk with family, a lot of times it was the two of us and the dog. After a leisurely meal he would spend two to three hours writing and reading. His big luxury was Wild West movies."* CK loved them because you can stop anywhere and yet catch up anytime without losing the action.

To his family's relief CK didn't take his work tensions home. He had his spaces well carved out. During conversation with family over dinner, CK would encourage his children to look at every problem and flip it on its head. *"Can we take a negative and make it a positive?,"* he would say.

Much before economists and the Indian government realized that its teeming population was an asset, not a curse, Deepa remembers her father talking about it in the 80s. CK would say: *"If you actually got all these people educated then you will have the greatest economic engine in the history of the world. The big question is how can you do it?"* She remembers that her father's passion was contagious. *"It wasn't just the outside world; his energy was brought inside the house too. And that was the great part of growing up with him; you could imagine what was possible."*

As the kids moved to college, CK would get them involved in his work as unofficial data gatherers and proof readers. He would engage his family the most when preparing his talks on India. It resembled a family enterprise then. To Gayatri, he was not just a great communicator outside but a great communicator at home as well.

Gayatri remembers her husband's revulsion to the idea of entitlement. He would give rewards for performance but never let the children think that it was an entitlement. At times, the reward would just be a 'I am so proud of you' and the negative feedback would just be a look that said 'I am disappointed.' He believed that to give a reward that is disproportionate would always result in unethical or dysfunctional behavior. CK told his children: ***"Let the world judge for who you are. You have to make things happen on your terms."***

Children learnt their ethics lessons from CK early on. To Murali, CK's son, it was a reboot of life in 1977 when they were told they'd be moving to the US. With four bags and only 28 dollars (only $7 per person was allowed by the government then), the family of four didn't care if the money they had was even enough to pay for the cab from the airport to the students' housing. It's not that they didn't have sufficient money to purchase US dollars in the black market.CK explained his decision by saying: ***"You don't start a new life through corrupt means. Whatever hell we go through you deal with it,"*** Murali recalls. His children were shown how one didn't follow ethics when it was easy. It should be followed when it was really painful.

Excellence is Painful

CK demanded very high academic performance from Murali and Deepa. He told them that they were the only Indians in their school and that the world should know that being Indian meant being excellent. When he saw things were not up to the mark, he would get very upset. They too hated to let him down. Murali went on to do his doctorate from Harvard University and chose to purse life sciences. Deepa later did her MBA from Tuck School of Business in the US.

CK's people skills were very original. He could be brutal with people he was close to. Murali says: *"When he really liked you he was brutal with you."* Being the older kid, Murali bore the brunt of it since Indian fathers usually dote on their daughters. Murali cannot forget his dad's reaction to his scores in the Japanese language paper. Murali had taken Japanese language in his first year of college and thought he was *"decently good"*. This was in 1988, the peak of the Japanese boom. CK was watching Japan very closely to see what India could learn from it. When Murali scored a 'C' grade, he tried giving all possible excuses including how hard it was to write the Japanese alphabet.

It didn't work. His father provoked him: *"Is a 2-year old Japanese kid smarter than you?"* He then asked him to go to his teacher and ask her to show him where he had gone wrong and write them down. *"I don't care if you have to keep writing till your hand falls off."* Murali followed what he'd been told and managed to get an 'A' in the next semester. Murali's learning from this episode was immense – no getting away with sloppy effort and that there was no alternative to hard work.

Yet, if the children got bad marks, CK was not upset. Gayatri recollects several situations where CK told them that it was okay if they got bad marks because that showed that they didn't understand and with some help that could be worked out. However, CK would get really upset if either of them got an A minus because he felt that they hadn't worked hard enough. 'Give 100 percent to everything you do' was CK's credo. He often told his family and friends, Gayatri recollects: *"In any relationship there was no fifty-fifty. If you give 100 percent to everything probably you will enjoy 200 percent of the benefits."*

It was clear to everyone that CK didn't believe in the much-debated concept of work-life balance. To him excellence was painful. *"You don't become great at anything by being balanced. To be excellent you have to be completely dedicated to whatever you are doing."*

People show their love and affection in different ways. People like CK belong to the kind that believes in being brutally honest even if it hurts. Not many could stomach it and some people even ended up misunderstanding him. That's a small price to pay, CK used to say, since very few take the risk of being truthful for fear of hurting someone or fear of being misunderstood.

Murali thinks CK was very situational in his approach. People who embraced it actually came back and said that was the best thing that happened to them. Some couldn't stomach it but he never tried to impose, at the same time he was encouraging and helpful. *"It wasn't so much about him but where you were at. He was blunt, the directness some people couldn't deal with it."*

Phenomenal success as one of the most sought after teachers and management consultants from global boards didn't make CK lax with his work ethic or integrity. It seemed excessive to a lot of his friends in the industry though. An instance of that was when less than a week before he passed away, CK asked for his cheque book to return the advance he had taken for speaking at a few conferences. He wrote a polite note expressing his difficulty.

He even turned down an invite from his old friend, Infosys founder Narayana Murthy, to join the company board saying he saw it as a conflict of interest because he was experimenting with a software venture of his own called *Praja*. No one really understood why he turned down consulting and board positions from Japanese auto companies. He felt, knowing well it was irrational, that he should be grateful to the place (Michigan, close to Detroit) which helped him build his career. This decision could have been very difficult because a resurgent Japan in the 1980s was giving American companies a run for their money. Toyota, Nissan and Mitsubishi were toppling Ford, GM and Chrysler from the top-seller charts.

It was in true CK style when he said: ***"In life you have to pick sides; you can't play all positions and be respected. There is something called morality and respect for the Western society, I am picking my side."***

CK consulted with several Indian companies and was on their board. He was careful to respect professional boundaries at all times. In one instance, at a top Tata company meeting, CK stood up to excuse himself when the board started to discuss products which Hindustan Lever produced. CK was on the Hindustan Lever board for a decade. CK used to say: ***"There is a line that you have to draw and nobody is going to do it for you. You have to have that discipline within yourself."***

One wondered if CK had any friends with his ultra-busy schedule of intensive teaching, extensive consulting with more than a dozen global and Indian companies and a punishing public-speaking schedule. CK knew he had to make some trade-offs if he had to focus on his high impact-driven goals. While he may not have had a typical buddy club to hang out with, CK charmed his colleagues, students and executives with his wit and hospitality. Dinners at his home in San Diego were sought after for their spread. CK had a knack for picking the best of wines and single malts. More than all that, people enjoyed what seemed like light-hearted conversations.

Tarun Das, Confederation of Indian Industry's Mentor, remembers a rather weird incident when CK had invited a few top business leaders to his home for dinner. The delegation arrived ten minutes late and CK was furious and he didn't hide it. He told them how they would never make it if they didn't respect time. Tarun Das let CK cool down before telling him that the delay was because the drivers of the car rental they had booked had lost their way. Tarun Das and CK go a long way. Mr. Das built the Confederation of Indian Industry brick by brick over three decades. It is the predominant industry body with influence on policy. Mr. Das offered CII as a platform to CK to explore his **'Transform Indian Business Mission.'**

Making friends came easily to CK. His enemies were typically not those he had harmed – typically they were those who thought his management ideas were too 'obvious' and that he did not deserve the rock star like following. Because of his hectic schedules CK didn't actively try to meet people. He used to say that his work was his calling card. He didn't take pride in who he knew; he wanted his work to speak for itself.

A creative contrarian with genuine humility is a potent cocktail, a rare blend. CK would say that humility keeps the pores of the skin open to signals in the environment. No wonder he had mastered the art of spotting weak signals and imagining the major trends that could emerge out of them over a period of time.

Stardom did not make CK inaccessible either. CK's famous line was **'you can break rules but don't break obligations.'** *"Every time we moved into a new house the first guest was always a professor who had picked us up from the airport, the first people who were there when nothing was certain,"* Gayatri remembers.

Deepa recollects how CK insisted on inviting the whole family of his friends and relatives to his talks across India. *"He was happy to discuss ideas with my cousins, most of them have asked him for career advice and he made time for them."* He gave priority to his old friends. Many of them, including his former colleagues in India Pistons turned up at the inauguration of CK's bust at the CII Centre in Chennai in 2012.

Pink Pearl Necklace

It looked like CK had a premonition of his death and wanted to thank a few people who had made his hectic life less hard on him. Two weeks before he was admitted to the hospital, he called Kiran Pascricha, CII's point person in the US, based in Washington DC, and asked her out for dinner. Kiran was surprised. It was a Sunday and dinner seemed a little odd. But she couldn't say no to CK.

CK didn't look too well. *"When CK's nose started to bleed I panicked, I didn't know he was that serious, nobody knew. I was horrified. He asked me not to worry. After a few minutes, he took out a pouch and there was this long double stringed pink colour pearls. He knew I always wore pink pearls. He said, 'This is from Gayatri and me to thank you for all that you have done for me.'"*

Kiran says her respect for CK is immense because *"I can't think even once where he made me feel like he was the guru and I was somebody small. He would carry his own bag, horrendously large bag and pay all his bills for years. He pushed himself too much, travelled too much."* Kiran now runs an annual CK Memorial Lecture in different cities in India each year.

MS Krishnan, CK's co-author and colleague at Michigan, remembered an incident when he was bowled over by CK's humility and patience. He and CK were in the Amsterdam airport in the middle of the night after flying some 9 hours from Mumbai. After a couple of hours in the lounge they were ready to take the flight back to Detroit. While going through security checks, one officer came up to CK and asked him if he was the CK Prahalad who had coined 'Core Competence'. CK said yes. And that he had written the book 'Competing for the Future'? CK said yes. The officer asked a few more questions and CK answered him patiently. It turned out that the officer was doing a part time MBA in Amsterdam. *"It was fascinating to see how he took time. Think about it; we are in the middle of these flights. That speaks a lot about CK in terms of his respect for individuals."*

Krishnan's respect for CK went up many more notches when he insisted on organizing a dinner for two administrators who had helped them with their book 'The New Age of Innovation' in the best restaurant in town. *"I learnt a lot at that dinner. He is special in terms of the attention he paid to individuals, recognizing their contribution."*

Another of CK's much loved traits was to make people completely at ease in a conversation and not letting his reputation come in the way. Once, Ted London, a colleague at Ross School of Business, had invited CK to have dinner with his family. *"He was very charming with them. He would talk about the things we were interested in. He would also engage my wife in a conversation and one of the things that really struck me was he made her feel very welcome in the conversation. My wife later told me she understood why everybody thought CK was so brilliant. Tonight, he made me feel like the smartest person in the world."*

So, what was CK really like as a person? Stuart Hart, CK's co-author of the famous article *'Fortune at the Bottom of the Pyramid'*, and CK's junior colleague who taught strategy at University of Michigan, has an interesting view. ***"CK was paradoxical – he was distant, yet incredibly warm; deadly serious (but) with a well-developed dry sense of humor; he travelled in elite circles, yet he also treated the secretaries, janitors and young professors with dignity and respect; he was dedicated to global impact, yet also cared deeply about the school, his colleagues, and his family."***

Marshal Goldsmith, celebrated author and executive coach and CK's neighbour at Rancho Santa Fe, California wrote in his obit in *BusinessWeek*: *"One of CK's passions was helping other thinkers develop. Each of his major books was co-authored with a different person. He was never threatened by his professional peers but always went out of his way to help them become better."*

Indian at Heart

Despite fame and money, first generation American citizens of Indian origin continue to have deep emotional attachment to India. For those who make an effort to look at India beyond its primitive infrastructure they genuinely wait for the day they can decide to get back. CK couldn't but be objective about everything. He couldn't hide his despair about India squandering its potential. Yet, he was patient and earnestly believed India would come out of its 'poor' status in everything it did to a shade closer to the best in his life time.

Deepa recalls: *"He was definitely a student of history; he loved looking at Indian culture and art. But he was not one of those who said our past was great therefore we are destined to be great. Ancient Greeks and Romans were also great. **The world respects accomplishment. If you don't do what you are supposed to do don't expect respect from what's been done by your ancestors.**"*

Murali is convinced his father was a serious student of history. *"He looked for the lessons, he looked for the patterns because I think he was of the view that even if history doesn't exactly repeat itself, it often rhymes."* CK ensured that his children were given exposure to Indian art and history. A visit to a historical place was part of their annual visit to India. He made them read what he thought they must know. He exposed them to the greatness of the Indian past; he wanted them to know how confident India was as a society; how wealthy it was to do the things it did; the complex systems and rules with which it worked.

CK compared the periods of Indian history with that of Europe in the second half of the last millennium to show how India was at par on architecture (the splendid Meenakshi Temple in Madurai was built around the same time as the famous cathedrals in medieval Europe) and had the second largest economy after China. CK's objective was to imbibe a sense of pride in India in his kids about the past as he didn't have much to be proud of the present. **CK tried telling them that the last 300 years were a blip in India's history and that it was destined for greatness again.**

CK wanted to see India as a developed country where poverty as we know now was extinct, it took pride in its past as well as what it did in the present, and exercised moral leadership globally which he thought was its heritage and responsibility, during his life time. While CK did what he could he has inspired a lot of people to believe in its immense possibility in the near future and has also shown a path. Perhaps, through this book many more will get inspired.

CK asked his family to immerse his ashes on the shores of Bay of Bengal in Chennai and in the sacred river Ganga. It was his tribute to the Bay of Bengal for taking him on an adventurous voyage across the seas and to Ganga for keeping him rooted to the idea of India.

Chapter 2

Go With Humility

I suggest to every student who is going on a mission to poor countries, I say go with humility, poor people know more about life than you will ever know. They suffer, they don't lose faith in themselves, so there is a lot more to learn and therefore pretending that you are educated is different from having wisdom which comes from long historical suffering. So if you can keep that in mind, we can create a new world. **CK Prahalad**

When GV Sanjay Reddy enrolled himself to do his Masters at the Ross School of Business, Michigan in 1987, he was pleasantly surprised to hear that an Indian professor had a major following among students. He was keen to attend this professor's class for a semester and gave his choice to the school office. The school had a system wherein students could choose a subject, and the teacher they preferred to teach that subject each semester. *"When I looked at the list of classes and professors who would teach them I was surprised to see that Prof. Prahalad's name was missing. Somewhat puzzled, I enquired at the office and was told that the school had a strange problem. Whenever they listed Prof. Prahalad's name, out of the 400 and odd students, everyone ticked his name as their first choice. The class capacity was only 80-90."*

Sanjay was disappointed. That made him more determined and the only way, he thought, was to gatecrash, in true Indian style. When he tried sneaking in, he was shocked to see nearly 200 students already there and no space even on the floor. Still he managed to slip in. *"CK did not make an issue about other students attending his class. I have never seen in my life a class which was bursting like this with students. There was no place even to walk, it was a great experience!"* Sanjay was happy that he got to attend CK's second class as well, this time from the front door.

He couldn't believe the stories he heard of CK's popularity right from the first year of his joining in 1977. CK had originally joined Michigan on a temporary posting as one of the professors had to take a break. When students heard that CK was there only to fill in for some-one for a year and that he would not be there to teach there anymore, they spoke to the administration, requesting that he stay on. When they said the rules did not permit that students went on a strike, a rare spectacle in an educational institution in the US. The authorities found themselves in an embarrassing position. They relented and CK was of-fered a full-time job. This meant a lot for CK as it gave him a strong foothold, an end to uncertainty and a platform from which he could launch his career.

The authorities' headache however didn't end there. University rules required a minimum of five years of teaching history before anyone even qualified for the prestigious annual *'Best Teacher'* award. But when the students gave CK the highest ratings in the very first year of his tenure, the authorities had no choice but to bend the rules. CK went on to win the *'Best Teacher'* Award several times in his career. **A very emotional CK told his wife Gayatri that his father would never have cared how much he was paid but would have been proud of the 'Best Teacher' Award.**

Sanjay came back to India to assist his father in running the Hyder-abad-based mega infrastructure-focussed GVK group. He says: *"At that time, I didn't know the impact CK had on me personally. But over the years,*

I have realized some of the things that he taught us and it is part of my business life. The most profound idea was how resource constraints should not limit the aspirations of entrepreneurs."

He and his father, GVK Reddy, seem to have followed CK's every word. From humble beginnings two decades ago, the GVK group today has emerged as one of India's leading infrastructure companies. They built the Nagarjuna Sagar Dam, the world's largest masonry dam; set up India's first independent power plant; laid India's first six-lane road project and they also rebuilt and currently operate the Mumbai and Bangalore airports. Perhaps their most audacious decision was their acquisition of a major Australian coal mine for $1.2 billion in November 2013. The group intends to invest $10 billion in mine, rail and port projects in the near future.

Venkatarama Raju, Managing Director of the Chennai-based Ramco Systems, was CK's student at Michigan in the eighties. He owes his tremendous success as a disruptor in the massive global enterprise resources planning (ERP) market to CK's seemingly simple, yet profound advice to all entrepreneurs. *"What he taught us again and again is that resource cannot be a constraint and therefore even small companies can challenge the giants if they have the vision and focus.... And the effectiveness of an enterprise can be gauged by its ability to give sustained great service despite continuous changes in the environment."*

Back to India, Mr. Raju had the audacious dream of starting an enterprise solutions company that could take on the giants in the business such as SAP and Oracle. *"This was an extremely ambitious vision and far beyond the capabilities and resources of a company like Ramco Systems. But our strength comes from our belief, which CK taught me – you cannot be marginally different and expect to compete with the big guys – you have to be radically different."*

Ramco has relentlessly pursued this line as one of India's pioneering product development companies for 20 years and now has a strong global footprint. Although it is yet to make money analysts believe that time is round the corner.

Nina Henning was peacefully managing a fair trade herbal products company in Nepal. But her life changed when she read *Fortune at the*

Bottom of the Pyramid'. She chose to enroll herself for an MBA at Michigan where CK was the star teacher. She says her best days were when she was part of a team that worked on a case study on Jaipur Rugs with CK as her advisor. CK's only brief to her and two other students, was to be humble and ask a lot of questions when they spoke to the artisans in rural Rajasthan. CK wanted them to understand how 40,000 artisans were able to produce a world-class product within a highly decentralized system of operations. This case study, along with a few more, was included in the revised edition of *'Fortune at the Bottom of the Pyramid'*.

The Ross School of Business had indeed spotted a rare gem, and CK repaid the school's trust for giving him the break when he needed it the most, with his loyalty. He served the school for 35 years – until his last day.

Seeing CK's popularity and the rave reviews of his articles, Harvard University and others offered him prestigious positions. When his family asked what he intended to do, CK told them: ***"Everybody will be nice to you when you are doing well, remember the people who were nice to you when you were not."***

Stuart Hart, CK's colleague at the Ross School of Business, remembers how CK's stardom as an author and a top consultant had made some of his colleagues jealous. They complained about his long absence from the campus even though he didn't miss any class. Gayatri remembers that the only day CK missed a class was when his mother passed away. CK felt that his work outside the campus enriched his teaching and research and the school management was supportive of his work. The school was aware how CK's brand helped the school and its Executive Education programmes.

Gayatri remembers her husband's condition to Philips that if he had a class they should fly him from their headquarters in the Netherlands to Michigan. Philips often sent him a private plane to teach the class, waited for him to finish and took him back. This was at a time when CK was deeply immersed in restructuring Philips in the early 1990s. (*See Chapter 5 -- 'Don of Business' for the fascinating story of the revival of Philips.*)

Talk to the Youth

One of the reasons students liked CK was because his finger was on the pulse on issues such as employment and social security. Amidst the surcharged interactions, CK didn't try to play down students' concern for job security and welfare. He used to say that if companies are to stay healthy and grow they had to make hard choices. Such statements confused students as to whether he was a capitalist or a socialist or to what extent he balanced the two. The labelling didn't matter to him. He wanted them to figure it out for themselves.

The 1970's, 80's and 90's were periods of virulent ideological conflict between capitalism, socialism, communism and their hybrids. Not many professors would take sides and feared talking openly to young people. CK was different. He used to say that he was not interested in what the academia thought of him. If what he said didn't appeal to the younger generation, it was a waste of time.

Once, CK was giving an interview to *Thinkers 50*, a respected global ranking of management thinkers, which had named him as the top global management guru in 2007 and 2009. The topic was *'Democratization of Commerce'*. As soon as the cameras were turned off, CK turned towards the cameramen and asked if they understood what he said, if it made any sense to them. This was his way of putting the theme of the interview into practice.

Once on a visit to his home town Coimbatore, he was asked to address 10,000 high school students. CK's son Murali remembers vividly how his father spent a lot of time preparing for it. *"Dad would get very irritated when people would come up to him casually and ask him to talk. He would say: 'People don't think I have to prepare'."* CK prepared for all his talks, it didn't matter who the audience was and he would be livid when other speakers didn't prepare well.

Gayatri still remembers her husband asking her to throw away all the notes he had prepared for the previous year's course. *"He would always make a new set of notes each year even if he was teaching the same case."* CK would tell her: **"If I repeat my notes, I will not be giving the best to my students. I will not be incorporating the new learning. The students won't know it, but I will."**

Prof. Kulkarni had taken over as the first Dean at IIM Ahmedabad when CK taught there for a brief period. CK was keen that a discussion shouldn't go haywire like most case study discussions do. Typically, after a class, professors say 'this session went off well,' but they rarely ask the students 'what did you learn'. ***Prahalad was very particular that at the end of each session you must learn something. Students looked happy after attending his class."***

Creative Contrarian

Case study-based teaching is an important part of MBA courses in business schools. They all teach almost the same case studies - about 25 to 30 great and failed American businesses – every year. While this is a convenient method for business schools to complete their curriculum quickly, students, and those who employ them, have been asking if they are really useful when they go out to face the real world. Business schools are at a loss to explain why so few entrepreneurs emerge from their portals and now, when even managers are required to have an entrepreneurial mindset to survive, are they really changing with the times?

One of the key reasons why organizations could be finding it so hard to adapt and remain agile is because they are run by managers who have been taught to learn from the past mistakes to manage current challenges and prepare for future challenges based on these lessons.

Students however remember CK's creative twists to popular case studies. Honda was everyone's favourite case because of its stupendous success in the US market for four decades. It was taught more as a marketing case study and this overlooked the more important reasons for its success.

Honda entered the American market after World War II. Its US advertising campaign, *'You meet the nicest people on a Honda'*, had a lasting impact on Honda's image and on American attitudes about motorcycling. Super Cub is reported to be the most produced bike in history with 60 million pieces up to 2008.

Just when students thought they had the case analyzed, CK would spring in to completely reorient their thinking. It turns out that Honda actually had no clue about what it wanted. It just happened to be a personal obsession of its founder Mr. Honda to rebuild the company. Desperate to keep his business alive, he sent a team of six engineers and product designers to Los Angeles in the early 1950s and told them to figure out for themselves what they wanted to do there. They had absolutely no idea what they were doing there for a long time. They didn't speak English and so the group preferred to stay indoors all the time. There was no TV then.

The group lived in a small flat in a densely populated poor suburb. Several months passed and they were getting tired of doing nothing. Mr. Honda didn't mind that. He told them to stay as long they wanted but they had to come up with a bright idea. To fight boredom they hung around car and bike showrooms and shopping malls.

One day, while lounging in their room, one of them blurted out- *"Could these poor guys buy a bike if they could afford one?"* That was their Eureka moment. The idea of an affordable bike was born and the rest, as they say, is history. The killer marketing and distribution strategy was not setting up or tying up with swanky auto dealers but with small retailers which their potential customers frequented almost every day. The lesson was clear - **bright ideas emerge from living among the people you want to serve.**

CK's style of teaching was intense. He had a playful style but he was tough at the same time. He would get a high treading on new frontiers and loved watching how they played out at the intersection of various dilemmas. He prepared to the last detail for his classes and talks and this required him to put in long hours. His family would, sometimes get frustrated about his insistence on doing everything himself. A teaching assistant to him was more of a bother, so he didn't have any in his long teaching career, something his peers couldn't comprehend. Gayatri, a Harvard graduate, says: *"He read every single student's paper. He even corrected full stops, commas and grammar. He felt the students were taking his class because they wanted his feedback and he didn't want to disappoint."*

'Creative contrarian' was a label CK didn't mind. It was evident right from his early days and in whatever he did, taught and wrote. **He taught his students to always look for the unintended consequences**

of any action - the 'toxic side-effects' as he liked to call them. He asked them to look at things through the 'other end of the telescope'.

It was important for CK that every class of his went off well. When it didn't, it would bother him no end. Gautam Ahuja, a fellow faculty member at the Ross School, remembers an incident which showed CK's incredible dedication to giving his best, which he says, left a big impact on him. *"He was coming over home for dinner with me after a class and I remember that for the entire three hours over dinner, he was extremely frustrated because some part of that MBA class that he had taken had not gone to his satisfaction. Now, I am pretty sure, any of the students would never even have noticed whether something went well or not. That's when I realized exactly how incredible he was as a teacher."*

A regular columnist for prominent publications like the Harvard Business Review, CK was a stickler for deadlines even if he was ill. CK even dictated a column for HBR to his daughter a few weeks before he passed away from his hospital bed.

Deepa remembers an instance. *"When I was in Singapore between 1996 and 1998 and wanted to book a restaurant for my going-away party, the hotel wasn't interested but when I gave my card which had Prahalad in it, the scene changed. The manager said that he had been to an executive program with my dad. He told her that* **everyone tried to teach him what he should do whereas CK made him believe what he could do.**"

Write for Yourself

It's funny how almost all students and executives CK taught have an interesting anecdote they love sharing. There's a certain spark in all of them when they say it. Many have become trail blazers and thought leaders in their domains. A majority of the entrepreneurs CK inspired are now leaders in their field. One wonders how it was possible for a teacher to profoundly influence so many people in a lifetime. And imagine if even few teachers try a little harder the world would be a better place.

A casual survey of what CK's students, entrepreneurs and executives have done with CK's advice makes for interesting reading. Rama

Bijapurkar, India's thought leader on consumer insights and their implication on business strategy, is an alumnus of IIM Ahmedabad where CK taught business policy in 1976-77. *"Though he taught me several years ago, he has been very generous with his time, counsel and wisdom through the years, in discussing the work that I was doing and helping me think further."* In the acknowledgements of one of her books, published after CK's demise, she says: *"CK Prahalad, my teacher at IIMA and mentor since, lives on in all the work that I do".*

She used to joke with him that she was like Eklavya, (a character in the epic Mahabharata), learning remotely from everything he wrote and said in his speeches. CK reminded her that he had never asked for her thumb (in the epic, Eklavya's teacher, Dronacharya demands that he cut off his thumb and present it to him as payment for his teaching). In her obit to CK, Rama wrote: *"But I can say with my hand on my heart that I would have willingly cut off my thumb had he asked for it, because he made such an enormous impression on my mind, and such an enormous impact on my work."* Instead of asking for her thumb, CK gave her a rule of thumb – **write for yourself if you want to articulate your ideas better.**

"To me that was paradigm changing advice. Suddenly, I understood that it was a struggle to write what I always thought I knew, because it's only when you actually put it together, that you begin to understand what you don't know." As a reward, CK promised to write a foreword if she got down to writing a book.

Rama wouldn't let go of this offer from a legend. *'We are Like that Only: Understanding the Logic of Consumer India'* in 2009 hit the stands and became a bestseller. CK not only wrote a nippy foreword, he also pointed out the gaps in editing and proof reading in her manuscript.

CK's foreword has a few powerful insights which could surprise those who have a stereotyped image of Indian consumer, including the 'educated' Indians. **He talks of how Indians may be poor, but they are not backward** (unlike the poor in most other countries); that they are not overwhelmed by western brands; that Indian consumers are well-informed even if access to media is patchy. He also praises Rama for developing a *"very strong case for learning about India on its own* *terms before investing."*

Her work busted many myths about the Indian consumer who has been patiently waiting to be understood in the cacophony of the Indian market place. Business school-bred MBAs, both foreign and Indian have had a simplistic view of the Indian consumer and when their strategies failed, sometimes repeatedly, they didn't even know who to blame. Rama was one of the first to ask CEOs not to look at India as a single market but to see it as one god with many heads. Rama has helped marketers know who their real customers are in the maze, and craft products to meet their specific needs. She has done this with workable frameworks and formulae making her book a must have for entrepreneurs and executives.

In the introduction to her second book *'A Never Before World: Tracking the Evolution of Consumer India'*, India's Finance Minister P Chidambaram observes that she 'approvingly' quotes (and builds on) CK Prahalad's most prophetic statement that **while it is true that multinationals will change emerging markets forever, the reverse is also true.**

In *'Customer in the Boardroom: Crafting Customer-Based Business Strategy'* Rama discusses how strategists could see the future unfold by invoking a fundamental lesson from Prahalad. One is that when one reads each signal of change individually, one runs the danger of strategists dismissing each signal as being too small or weak to be of much consequence. However, when several of these small changes are read together, they send out a clear and loud signal of a change about to happen.

She sums it up; *"Thank God for CK Prahalad. But for him, simple truths would not be acknowledged across boardrooms around the world – that people with less money desire all the same things that people with more money do, but do not buy them because they cannot afford them. And growth strategists would not have known the* **idea of a price-performance point which enables both customer happiness and business profitability. In the absence of this insight, we would still be trapped in the** *'tyranny of OR' – customer happiness OR business profitability."*

Reinventing Research

Like in everything else, CK had a different approach to the how and what of research. He believed that as a researcher one must push oneself into zones of discomfort, and not coast along with what one knows. In his interview to Lynn Perry Wooten and Anne Parmigiani of the University of Michigan and Nandini Lahiri of the Indian School of Business in the Journal of Management Inquiry, June 2005, CK said: *"And I was not necessarily motivated by doing things you would characterize as main line of research. After a lot of soul searching, I decided that thinking about how things happen is more interesting for me than thinking about what are the broad patterns and developing generalizations, which is what most research is. Because it's history! By the time you collect a lot of data, things have already happened, and the research focusses on history rather than asking the question,* **'How is the future being created?'** *If* **you want to understand how the future is being created, you have to understand how decisions get made, how people allocate resources, how choices get made."**

CK's advice to students wanting to write research papers was blunt: **"If you believe deeply in something, you must be persistent. If you follow what others want you to do, you're playing the game according to their rules. You will never win. Play the game according to your rules. This is rule number one in strategy. Invent a new game, and there will be a lot of room at the top of the field for you.** *The bottom is crowded. If you're a strategist, your job should be to get to the top as fast as possible. And it is not possible to get to the top if you're doing standard mainstream research because there is just too much competition. If you're the first to find some new big problem where nobody's working on it, you're the only game in town. So the question is how to do it? Find the only game in town that is the right game for you, and this is the one that you can get passionate about!"*

CK went on to create a framework that helped understand the tension between forces of global integration of firms and the responsiveness of the local environment. He used the same work to understand the drivers of organizational structure and processes. *"In other words, here was a framework by which you could understand the nature of the business underlying economics and also understand the require-*

ments of the internal organization." **This framework was one of the first in strategy research to integrate industry analysis with organizational analysis.**

What intrigued CK most in the eighties was how a few small firms in Asia were threatening the monopoly of large American and European firms. His research into this phenomenon, along with a doctoral student at the University of Michigan Gary Hamel, led to the bestseller *'Competing for the Future'.* The book broke several deeply held strategy research and practice myths. CK said: *"First, the notion of 'fit' was central to strategy. But entrepreneurship is not about fit. Strategy must be about stretch. Second, this created the notion that* **aspirations must be, by design, outside your resource base."**

The book's findings showed that you don't have to have all the resources to be a world leader. *"You can create resources; you can leverage resources. Therefore, it was about hope and about entrepreneurship and about regeneration of tired companies."*

To CK global poverty was not a theoretical construct and not a number. He had a visceral understanding of what it is to meet with people who were poor. One of his most profound questions that he asked himself was: ***"Are five billion people so disenfranchised that we have no answers to that problem?"*** His next big question was, *"How do I create the enabling conditions for the poor to have access to credit and products and services that could help them realize their aspirations, which, in fact, are the same as that of the rich and the middle class?"* The result was his book *'Fortune at the Bottom of the Pyramid'.*

If there had been a prize for the most rejected papers going on to win the best paper awards, CK would have won it hands down. Two of his award winning papers *'Dominant Logic'* and *'Strategic Intent'* were rejected by the Journal of Marketing and Harvard Business Review initially. Even his paper on the *'Bottom of the Pyramid'* was rejected by HBR and gathered dust for two years. It was later published in a lesser known journal, *strategy+business.* The article was then expanded into a book with the same name and first published in 2004. This book sells more copies every year, even now, than most new business management books.

Go with Humility

Just like CK made Indian business leaders think beyond business, he made his students think beyond degrees and got them to think about impacting society. To get students to do this, teachers have to create intellectual excitement among students which, his students say, CK did with ease.

Typically, the first six months of a one-year course with CK was spent in 'forgetting'. *"You have to forget before you learn something,"* was part of his initial remarks at the beginning of every course. The biggest turn on for his students was the possibility of being part of the intellectual leadership of creating opportunities. CK's standard message to students, especially after he got subsumed by the historic possibilities of the bottom of the pyramid idea -- *"This experience is for those of us who are willing to go and spend time, to be humble enough and to be open enough. Without openness of mind we cannot learn from these models. I suggest to every student who is going on a mission to poor countries, I say go with humility, poor people know more about life than you will ever know. They suffer, they don't lose faith in themselves, so there is a lot more to learn and therefore pretending that you are educated is different from having wisdom which comes from long historical suffering. So if you can keep that in mind, we can create a new world."*

Sure enough, CK's students remember him less for unleashing their imagination about immense possibilities without worrying much about constraints. **In a way, he set them free.** They stepped into the tough world of business not to find jobs but to pursue a mission. While it seemed daunting to them initially, most students have gone on to build highly profitable and responsible companies and institutions.

Chapter 3

Teacher's Teacher

CK's most radical and contrarian idea was that business has a deep and inescapable moral obligation to the world's poor. There are several billion people in this planet who owe CK a debt for driving that point home again and again in boardrooms and conferences all around the world. **Gary Hamel**

CK's professional life was a case study in what it takes to multiply your impact for good in the world. **Gary Hamel**

Stuart Hart did his Masters at Yale School in Forestry and Environmental Studies in the 1970s. He can't clearly remember how he ended up in a doctoral programme in strategic decision-making and then got into Ross School of Business in Michigan teaching strategy where CK was a senior faculty member. But even after settling down to a comfortable teaching job for five years or so, the environment bug didn't really go away. He tried hard to get Environment into mainstream strategy discussions, but was frustrated because he didn't get enough support.

Almost everyone in the school told him that if he persisted with his pet idea and obsession, it could destroy his career. They told him to settle down by getting tenure, to write articles and be happy. Stuart Hart was confused between settling for a comfortable teaching career and chasing his passion. He went to CK expecting him to understand his dilemma since he was known for his radical approach to everything. Hart recollects CK telling him: *"How could there be any other choice? You have to go with your passion; if you don't do it you will look back 30 years from now and you will never forgive yourself. If you just buckle under and comply, you could end up never forgiving yourself, you have to do this."*

Hart says: *"CK was actually very important in giving me that empowerment that I could make the personal choice to go this route and the hell with everybody else. He gave me the courage to take this step. In 1990, I consciously made a decision to devote my life to Environment; it's the best decision of my life."*

As his peers expected, Stuart Hart's career began faltering at Ross School. His tenure was on hold because he had not published articles in prominent journals. But there was help. CK saw that Prof. Hart had a point of view in his paper *'Beyond Greening, Strategies for a Sustainable World'* and introduced him to the editor of the Harvard Business Review. The article went on to win the McKinsey Award for Best Article in 1997 and helped launch **the movement for corporate sustainability.**

By now, the two colleagues had built up enough kindred spirit which helped them in exploring newer paths together. They sat down and wrote *'The Strategies for the Bottom of the Pyramid'*, how MNCs should view the developing world as their future growth market with innovative price points instead of trying to milk their own saturated markets. This article also provided the first articulation of how business could profitably serve the needs of the four billion poor in the developing world.

They were thoroughly excited about the game-changing possibilities of this article and sent it to HBR in 1998. When they did not hear from the usually professional editorial team of the magazine for months, they were upset and wondered what could have gone wrong. It was more than two years since their submission and they couldn't wait any longer. When they persisted, HBR replied that the article was too radical and that it did not follow the work of developmental economists. The publisher and the editor were not sure the article would work since it didn't have any multinational success story in it. An annoyed CK retorted: *"That's the point! It was not about looking backward but looking at the future about what could be."*

Booz & Company's *strategy+business* was then relatively a new magazine then and was serious about breaking the stranglehold of HBR over management publishing. Its editor was open to new ideas but wasn't sure if the original title would draw readers to it. He insisted on a more flashy title and the authors had to relent even if they thought the word 'fortune' could be misleading. The article finally got published with the title *'Fortune at the Bottom of the Pyramid'* in January 2002. It was a typical author-editor stand-off and the editor won, much to the authors' displeasure. But when it surprisingly worked, they stopped complaining.

Once they agreed to the new title, CK told Hart not to worry and that he would do his best to minimize the damage. CK anticipated the critics' potshots. He wrote blogs and travelled extensively asking people to read the article fully and not selectively as some critics were doing. Their biggest fear was if critics interpreted it as *'There's a big bag of money at the base of the pyramid, let's go get it'*. And whether *'fortune really meant foretelling and executives would think there is big money to be made in the future'*.

Hart and CK were nearly the same age but were worlds apart in everything else. **"What I learnt from CK the most was his ability to turn things on their head. He was the master of that, just when you think you have the case analyzed, CK would spring a surprise and completely reorient your thinking."**

Since then, Hart pursued his passion and has emerged as one of the leading global thought leaders in Sustainability. He co-founded the Emergent Institute in Bangalore in 2011, his first big initiative to engage with entrepreneurs in developing sustainable products and strategies to market them globally.

CK stuck to what he knew best – business strategy. By the late 1980s, CK had made a name with his book on *'Core Competence'* and an HBR article in 1989 titled *'Strategic Intent'* both with Gary Hamel, who taught at the London Business School. The two publications set the management and business world abuzz.

Big Picture Man

Academicians who have worked closely with CK, and those who have watched him from a distance, remember CK's simple yet profound statements like – *'You should never think you know everything'*. A counterintuitive approach to everything was in his DNA. And when articulated in his baritone voice, the idea amplified several fold – something which students craved for in his classes, and got!

Unfortunately, even if he wanted to, CK had no time for mentoring junior faculty or students. He spent most of his time on the big picture and set out to solve the problems of the world and that of India in particular. ***"You don't get to practice sitting in your office, spinning secondary data, analyzing it, that doesn't get you there,"*** was one of his favourite lines. Not many could gather the courage to approach CK because he came across as aloof and removed and hard to accept. But once he knew someone was committed, he could be extremely generous.

Yves Doz, Solvay Chair Professor of Technological Innovation at INSEAD, worked with CK to fix a major problem of a large European company. Prof. Doz cannot forget the demanding work schedule CK subjected him to. *"Naively I thought that by 6 PM the day was done. Not at all; it was starting. CK would say, 'let's figure out what we learnt today' and the conversation would continue even after dinner. Finally by 2 or 3 AM, we would call it quits. We were basically working from 8 in the morning till 3 in the morning, just about every night."*

*"That's the level of commitment CK showed especially to research projects. A few things that really struck me was CK's patience with research – he was not someone who would run and try to do a quick job. **And there was this constant interplay between getting more data, more information, taking the leadership of the conversation without taking the direction of the conversation.** That was a magnificent lesson for me."*

They went on to co-author *'The Multinational Mission: Balancing Local Demands and Global Vision'* in 1987.

It's Possible to Make an Extraordinary Difference

Gary Hamel and CK had a very intense professional relationship – as co-authors, family friends and provocateurs. Interestingly, they started as sparring partners at a doctoral seminar early in their careers in Ross School of Business, when Hamel was a doctoral student and CK a new faculty member. They may have had a few bouts occasionally after that, but together have produced some of the most radical, rich and game-changing literature in business and management in the last three decades. (*See Chapter 7 –'Distilling CK – A Critique of his Published Work' for a full discussion of their work*).

Hamel, who moved to London Business School from Michigan, says: ***"CK's professional life was a case study in what it takes to multiply your impact for good in the world."*** CK told Gary that he was far more interested in making a difference than making a career.

What does it really take for someone to make a difference? The first and most fundamental quality is courage, which Hamel thinks CK was not short of. Courage involved not worrying about whether what you say or do will affect your career. *"He wrote in places that didn't bring in a lot of academic credit or glory. He spent a lot of time inside large complex organizations where he wanted to test his ideas and see if they met the real challenges."* It also involved contesting powerful beliefs.

CK was intrigued by daunting problems like **how to revitalize a large company or how do you bring the fruits of capitalism to the poor.** He was very sure that it was hard to make a difference unless you were willing to work on hard problems and that life was too short to work on anything else. **CK's most radical and contrarian idea was that business has a deep and inescapable moral obligation to the world's poor.** It also meant that what was good for humanity could ultimately be good for business as well. In his tribute to CK, Hamel said: *"There are several billion people in this planet who owe CK a debt for driving that point home again and again in board rooms and conferences* *all around the world. Today that idea is no longer radical, no longer exceptional, it simply makes sense."*

People close to CK were astonished at the crazy level of energy he had. Hamel noted: ***"That kind of stamina comes only if you really believe that you are doing God's work. I learnt from him that making a difference requires a courageous heart, a contrarian spirit, a compassionate soul and that any professional qualification, even intellectual brilliance, will not be a substitute for those things."***

After writing many bestselling books and several award-winning articles, Hamel started to focus on consulting and writing on the future of Management. He set up a firm called *Strategos* to bridge the gap between academic theory and real-world practice in 1995.

While CK didn't cut back on teaching, he shifted his focus to making a deep impact at the intersection of business and society. The outcome of this detour was the *'Fortune at the Bottom of the Pyramid'* and two other books with Indian co-authors– *'The Future of Competition: Co-creating Unique Value with Customers'* with Venkat Ramaswamy and *'The New Age of Innovation: Driving Co-created Value Through Global Networks'* with MS Krishnan.

It certainly looks like Gary Hamel has a lot of fire left in his belly. He launched *Management Lab* (MLab), along with a few partners, as a non-profit corporation, based in California, with a mission to accelerate the evolution of management by bringing together some of the world's leading business thinkers, academics, executives, institutions and organizations. In fact, CK went for one of its retreats in 2009. It would be great if he can take some of CK's unfinished agenda forward, especially in the area of sustainability and innovation as the frontiers of Business and Management.

Reinvent or Retard

Each of CK's four colleagues and co-authors at the Ross School of Business – MS Krishnan, Ted London, Gautam Ahuja and Venkat Ramaswamy, can't help but relive their short tryst with the intellectual giant. Gautam Ahuja, who teaches Strategy, couldn't help notice CK's 'incredible curiosity.' ***"He was always asking questions. I was amazed by his 'democracy of opinion' which he used to either validate or negate a point of view."***

CK's colleagues wondered how he could converse with drivers, security agents, receptionists or a janitor with ease. *"By the time he is talking to a CEO, he already has six opinions on the ground of what the world looked like. He already had these perspectives, so I think a clear part of it was his curiosity, his willingness to take thoughts in from everybody. He didn't just let the thoughts stay in his mind; he tried to build a point of view around those thoughts."*

Writing down thoughts in whatever form they are – fully processed, half baked, fleeting, was CK's secret to discovering fresh insights. This discipline's reward is that when you observe anything that may seem pedestrian to others, you are able to spot interesting trends. The discipline of simply talking, writing and observing, CK believed, was enough to make anyone intelligent.

"I think that's an incredible lesson that he left behind for all of us in the academics business - **the underlying idea that a worst written paper still has a better chance of getting published than the best unwritten one.** *I remember that once after a long day, he said: 'I have to go and write.' I was thinking I have to go and sleep!"* Prof. Ahuja feels these were the incredible parts of the puzzle that allowed CK to be a dominant force in Management teaching and writing for three decades.

A compulsive belief in reinventing oneself all the time drove CK to achieve extraordinary feats. Venkat Ramaswamy says: *"He had this desire to think about what the future might look like. He used to always talk about folding the future in, which was one of his pet ways of thinking about 'next practices', which I thought, was a brilliant term. One of the things that struck me in collaborating with him was that he used to stretch your imagination – How do you get from here to there, and his ability to challenge the status quo all the time."*

Published in 2004 by Harvard University Press, *The Future of Competition* with Venkat Ramaswamy is considered visionary. Its central theme, as described on the cover is: *"In a world in which information is readily available to everyone, the role of the customer has changed dramatically. Once passive recipients of the products and services companies created for them –* *customers are now active participants who actually co-create the value they receive, from products and services they help develop, test, and distribute."* Some believe this book could have been the trigger for Facebook and other social media platforms where the content is generated by the users.

There's a popular saying that nothing grows in the shadow of giant trees. Prof. Ramaswamy says CK was just the opposite. *"He never imposed his views on anybody. You had to win him over by presenting an equally good or better view and if you did that he was open to listen (to you). But if you failed he didn't hold it against you. He just went his own way.* ***He never pushed himself as the only true voice of a field or a department and for that we specially value him."***

MS Krishnan and CK co-authored *'The New Age of Innovation – Driving Co-created Value Through Global Networks'*. It was published in 2008 by McGraw-Hill. This was CK's last book. Prof. Krishnan says: ***"It was important for him that you should have clarity in your point of view and then you build tolerance for other people's point of view."*** This book's timing was spot on because the internet and social media were making disruption a rule rather than an exception and businesses were at sea.

The 2008 recession has forced business leaders and gurus to rethink the very fabric on which organizations are built and run. S Ramadorai, Vice Chairman of Tata Consultancy Services, couldn't have said it better – *"Prahalad and Krishnan show us how innovation will be driven by the seamless integration of strategy, business process, technology and people. While this may seem an insurmountable task, the authors delight the reader by creating an architectural framework for business transformation. I have yet to come across a book that offers such a clear roadmap."*

When you wonder how someone reinvents himself, it is implicit that you give up what you had first. But giving up is very easy when you fail the first time but the real challenge is to give up when you have succeeded enormously, that's when it becomes nearly impossible to reinvent yourself. Gautam Ahuja says: *"The reason why many academics don't go beyond the first or second idea is not because they don't have the intellectual capacity but success becomes a barrier in their thinking further because it's difficult to let go of something worthy; its already made you famous so why not flog it one more time. What was amazing about him (CK) was that he did it, succeeded, went beyond all expectations, became a superstar and dropped it to take on something new. He made this a habit."*

The list is long -- *dominant logic, core competence, strategic intent, future of competition, bottom of the pyramid.* Prof. Ahuja is certain CK could do this because he had a natural entrepreneurial instinct in him. **Only a person who has abundant appetite for risk taking can do this.**

Ted London, like Stuart Hart and Eric Kacou (author of *'Entrepreneurial Solutions for Prosperity in BoP Markets: Strategies for Business and Economic Transformation'*), belongs to the bottom of the pyramid evangelists' circle. He co-authored *'Next Generation Business Strategies for the Base of the Pyramid: New Approaches for Building Mutual Value'* with Stuart Hart, in which CK was to have a chapter. CK was fighting for his life in the early months of 2010 and consequently, could not contribute his chapter.

Stuart Hart and Prof. London are working very hard to take the BoP (Bottom of the Pyramid) model to the next level by extending it to the Sustainability platform. In fact, their book offers new techniques based on the crucial lessons learnt by BoP pioneers and shares lessons that dramatically increase the likelihood of success of future BoP ventures.

Prof. London, a colleague of CK at the Ross School, is one of the very few experts in the industry who focusses on designing enterprise strategies and poverty-alleviation approaches for low-income markets, developing capabilities for new market entry, building cross-sector collaborations, and assessing the poverty-reduction outcomes of business ventures. His book on the Acumen Fund's experience in funding such ventures is illuminating.

Having seen CK's magic, Prof. London is amazed at how a man could do so much – *"To have these conversations, it sounds kind of easy but to have both scholarly written conversations and actual in-person conversations across this huge swath of humanity is pretty amazing. Because to have the ability to ask the right questions, to listen, to continue a dialogue where people want to talk to you and do it in all these different domains is an incredible trait that very few people have."*

More importantly, he adds: ***"Some people can stay in consulting and be very good in that, or academia or writing cases; CK could transcend all of this. The ability to really listen, and when he is having those conversations, he is respecting those people."***

Where's the Open Culture?

One wonders why management gurus rarely dialogue or debate or even critique one another in public forums or in journals. One thought that America's bedrock is its open culture – even its presidential candidates slug it out on television before the elections. Stuart Hart was taken aback by this question when asked by the author during an interview for the book. He mumbled: *"No, the culture is more to steer clear of each other because they have their own space, their own ecosystem. It doesn't really benefit them to go after each other; they don't really collide with each other. The world is a big enough space."*

Another perplexing trend among management gurus/consultants is not acknowledging earlier works when they publish their books whose central themes are clear extensions of usually well-received books. When pressed by either the family of the author or a stubborn journalist, they are known to acknowledge it in private. CK's *'Fortune at the Bottom of the Pyramid'* has had many clones in recent years. It's shocking to see the authors not acknowledging the original work even as inspiration.

Management's biggest challenge today is to show that it is still relevant by coming up with effective models and solutions to global problems like climate change, affordable healthcare and education, among others. In a way, Management theorists and practitioners have the responsibility to transform businesses and societies from a gloomy future to one of optimism for the next generation. **CK has shown academia that seeking to make an impact at the highest level has to be academia's most important goal.**

Prof. Bala V Balachandran, Dean and Founder of Great Lakes Institute of Management and Kellogg Distinguished Professor of Accounting was CK's friend and contemporary. To him *"CK's clarity of thought and creative expression created lasting impression. While his peers were focussing on publishing papers and researching technical concepts and analytical processes, CK rightly realized the importance of impact at the highest level."*

Be a Sheep Dog, not a Shepherd

Leaders must lead. You cannot lead unless you are future oriented; leadership is about the future; it's about the point of view of the future, and it's about hope. The first thing is we must have a distinct point of view, not about our current affairs, but how the world can be ten years from now.
CK Prahalad

Metaphors are a teacher's best tool. It helps them convey complex ideas even to the less gifted. CK's favourite metaphor was that of a sheep dog when he spoke to senior executives at executive education workshops. **A sheep dog has to follow certain rules – it is always behind; it can bark a lot but can't bite; it cannot lose any sheep; and it should know where it is going.**

CK felt the sheep dog metaphor was better than the shepherd metaphor because shepherds can be anywhere and assume that they are ahead of the sheep. He told an interviewer: *"The reason I am saying this is when talent becomes the critical resource for running companies and is distributed around the world, inter cultural competence, inter personal competence, the capacity to get people from different parts of the world from China, India, Germany, UK, US and Brazil all to work together requires the ability of a good sheep dog."* It also involves: *"How to talk to people constantly, motivate them, how to get them to see the tasks on hand and how to reduce the frictional losses in pulling people together from multiple cultures, that becomes a dominant theme. So it's not the great man view of leadership, it is somebody who gets you to be as good as you can be."*

At a time when 'leadership' has become the most talked and written about subject with newer concepts and varieties, CK's version will remain fresh for a long time and puts immense responsibility on leaders. CK said: *"Leaders must lead. You cannot lead unless you are future oriented; leadership is about the future; it's about the point of view of the future,* *and it's about hope. **The first thing is we must have a distinct point of view, not about our current affairs, but how the world can be ten years from now.** That is the first principle of a good leader."*

CK deliberately taunted global leaders when he said: *"I am arguing strategy and leadership is not extrapolating the current situation to the future but imagining the future and folding that future in."*

In his long career at Citibank, Jerry Rao attended several executive education programmes but he remembers CK's as the most powerful. *"CK's was the most participative, least preachy and the one that provided the most challenging strategic content, not just focus on process."*

Then what credit should CK get for the spectacular success of Indian business in the last 25 years? Jerry feels catalysts' impact are always very difficult to measure. *"There's so much statistical white noise. The fact that all these guys together got it means something, doesn't it?"*

Executive education has matured and is in the reinvention stage in the US and UK but is relatively a recent phenomenon in India. Its potential is largely unexplored. CK was committed to making Michigan a global leader in it. He built much of Ross School's executive or management development effort across the world and used his network in India to the maximum. The Tatas, Mahindras, Godrej, ICICI Bank, TVS and a few other groups used Ross School professors to train their senior executives initially in Michigan and later on their campus.

Jerry, like CK, is a Loyola College Chennai, and IIM Ahmedabad alumnus. He is today one of India's star serial entrepreneurs. After selling his BPO company MphasiS to HP, he now runs Value and Budget Housing Corporation – a bottom of the pyramid concept with the ambition of building one million budget homes in a decade.

CK gave Jerry a *"hard time"* for not using his original name Jaithirth, which he said was such a nice name, instead of an Americanized Jerry. Jerry remembers, even after a decade, what CK told him about strategy **– that strategic planning does not require it to be very complicated. That it was common sense most of the time and companies waste too much time and money and effort on the obvious.**

CK was not known for being kind with the confused. *"He used to repeatedly tell us that - If you can't be a low cost producer; you go, do something else. If you are not sure of risks then don't be in business, it's not a monastery."*

CK talked about the importance of what signals organizations gave to talent as more important than a written down code - If we want talented people to work on a project the signal you send has to be that if you work there you get promoted faster. But if they see that only finance guys get promoted, you will see that in two years or so good talent in project management will disappear – *"You have to give the right signal to talented people. If you want to attract them give them real career breaks then automatically talent will come."*

CK scoffed at Indian businesses if they asked for a discount in his fees for workshops or talks. He would tell them that if they could pay big money to American consulting firms, how could they make a fuss to pay him? He would tell them bluntly; *"I may kill myself and do more. I am trying to get you to the top where you can compete with the rest of the world, accept it or don't, but these are my rates."*

Partners' Program

The Partners' Program was CK's master stroke. MS Krishnan, faculty member at the Ross School and CK's right hand man in this venture and co-author, says CK used to constantly innovate in the delivery of the programme. For example, CK recognized the fact that senior executives were spending 2-3 weeks away from their families and to make them comfortable he launched the 'Partners Program'. Playing on the spouses' pride factor, he ensured that the same faculty taught at both programmes but the wives' ones were shorter. CK joked saying spouses needed only two days, not two weeks to learn because they had less to forget.

CK saw executives as humans first and employees next. Although he personally didn't believe in work-life balance, he understood that managers led stressful lives and it's important that learning centres maintained a relationship with the family. Gayatri Prahalad often helped with the partner programme. CK almost made the executive programmes a family affair, which appealed to executives.

At a breakfast meeting in 2004, CK invited MS Krishnan to serve as the Faculty Director for executive programmes in India. Krishnan remembers CK telling him in a no-nonsensical tone; *"That this is not a transactional relationship; this is not about how many programmes we do; or think in terms of what is the impact you are going to create. This has to be a transformational experience for you and the way we take Michigan to India and how you impact the companies in India."*

If annual CEO Forums were CK's nurseries where he groomed Indian business leaders to blossom into global players, in Executive Education workshops he turned managers into confident generals.

CK's 11 Commandments for Responsible Managers

1. Understand the importance of nonconformity. Leadership is about change, hope, and the future. Leaders have to venture into uncharted territory, so they must be able to handle intellectual solitude and ambiguity.

2. Display a commitment to learning and developing yourself. Leaders must invest in themselves. If you aren't educated, you can't help the uneducated; if you are sick, you can't minister to the sick; if you are poor, you can't help the poor.

3. Develop the ability to put personal performance in perspective. Over a long career, you will experience both success and failure. **Humility in success and courage in failure are hallmarks of a good leader.**

4. Be ready to invest in developing other people. **Be unstinting in helping your colleagues realize their full potential.**

5. Learn to relate to those who are less fortunate. Good leaders are inclusive, even though that isn't easy. Most societies have dealt with differences by avoiding or eliminating them; few assimilate those who aren't like them.

6. Be concerned about due process. **People seek fairness – not favours.** They want to be heard. They often don't even mind if decisions don't go their way as long as the process is fair and transparent.

7. Realize the importance of loyalty to organization, profession,

community, society, and above all, family. Most of our achievements would be impossible without our families' support.

8. Assume responsibility for outcomes as well as for the process and people you work with. **How you achieve results will shape the kind of person you become.**

9. Remember that you are part of a privileged few. That's your strength, but it's also a cross you carry. **Balance achievement with compassion and learning with understanding.**

10. Expect to be judged by what you do and how well you do it – not by what you say you want to do. However, the bias toward action must be balanced by empathy and caring for other people.

11. Be conscious of the part you play. Be concerned about the problems of the poor and disabled, accept human weaknesses, laugh at yourself – and **avoid the temptation to play God**. Leadership is about self-awareness, recognizing your failings, and developing modesty, humility, and humanity.

Excerpt from CK Prahalad's article in Harvard Business Review Jan-Feb 2010 titled 'Responsible Manager'

Chapter 4

Indian CEOs --
Turning Sheep into Tigers

CK was gathering us like a shepherd would gather his flock of sheep and was essentially bent on chastising us for what we hadn't done and how and what we could do. **Anand Mahindra, Vice Chairman of Mahindra & Mahindra**

What does it take for Indian companies to globalize and the risks that you take and its opportunities were discussed extensively in CEO sessions. This really inspired me to make the first trans-border acquisition of Tetley. **Krishna Kumar, former Director, Tata Sons**

He made business leaders think big, imagine the impossible and chase it as if it was no big deal. **Dr. Sridhar Mitta, first CTO of Wipro, currently Chairman, NextWealth Entrepreneurs Private Limited**

While we were so much engulfed by gloom that everything appeared like a big challenge, he had the ability to pull you out of that and show you what lies ahead. **Kalpana Morparia, CEO, J P Morgan Chase**

CK's faith in Indian manufacturing was honey to my ears. A lot of us used to think, after looking at China, that India had no future in manufacturing. But CK made us think big. Because of him we started believing that manufacturing is not necessarily about repeatability, not only about scale. It is also about innovation. His inspiration led us to seek the Deming Prize and we got it. **B Muthuraman, former MD, Tata Steel**

CK arrived a few minutes early. A stickler for time, he was annoyed as the chatter wouldn't end and people were still ambling in. As they were settling down, in his baritone voice, CK's opening line was: *"You all have gotten used to people carrying your bags and you walk with a sense of entitlement. All that could soon end."* Even before he completed his sentence, a senior ITC executive walked in with his assistant carrying his bag. The room burst into loud laughter. The ITC man looked amused and half-guessed that the joke probably was on him. The mood lightened up.

On a cool January morning in 1994, more than thirty Indian top business owners huddled around Prof. CK Prahalad in Westminster, a conference room in the British Raj style five star hotel, ITC Windsor Manor in Bangalore. They had no clue why the popular India-born American management guru had called them personally. Curiosity and anticipation filled the air.

CK had picked his group carefully. Some of them were his students at the Ross School of Business, University of Michigan. He had also invited several heads of top business houses, many of them in their thirties and early forties. They looked like they were raring to go, but felt marooned when the floodgates of the economy were opened for global competition in 1991. CK could sense a strange mix of gloom and hope on their faces.

The first day of the Bangalore CEO Forum, popularly referred to as the Windsor Club, may well be one of the most defining moments in India's modern business history. It was here that a teacher, in the words of Anand Mahindra, Vice Chairman of Mahindra & Mahindra: *"He was gathering us like a shepherd would gather his flock of sheep and was essentially bent on chastising us for what we hadn't done and how and what we could do."*

Defining moments are seldom forgotten. For someone with Anand Mahindra's intensity, they haunt him. He says: *"The Bangalore sessions were like a locker room of an American football team with the coach coming in, screaming at you for your pathetic show but at the same time describing the mission, telling you what lay ahead of you, how victory could be achieved, then giving you a pat on the back before you went out on the field."* KV Kamath, Chairman of ICICI Bank concurs: *"He was so sharp in his criticisms that it was like a punch in the gut."*

The turnout list was impressive. KV Kamath, N Vaghul, (founder of ICICI Bank), Anand Mahindra, Adi Godrej, Azim Premji (Chairman of Wipro), Gopal Srinivasan and Venu Srinivasan (TVS), Jairam Varadaraj (Elgi), Venkatarama Raju (Ramco Systems), Shiv Nadar (HCL), CEOs from the Murugappa Group and the Amalgamations Group, Sridhar Mitta and Ashok Soota, then with Wipro, Krishna Kumar and a few other senior Tata Group CEOs and many more. This group attended almost all of the five three-day annual retreats CK held in Bangalore between 1994 and 1999. The forum then shifted to Mumbai's Taj Mahal Hotel where CK held an annual session until 2009 with one session in Chennai somewhere in between.

This is an action-packed chapter where top Indian business leaders live out their experience of the mental gymnastics CK subjected them to, the 'exorcism' tricks he used on them to rid them of their dark spirits, their key learnings, what they unlearnt and how they went on to build globally competitive and strong enterprises in just over a decade.

Inside-Out Approach

Rampant mismanagement, short-sighted political leadership and the trademark Indian trait of waking up only when pushed into a deep crisis had brought the Indian economy to the brink in 1991. With foreign reserves barely enough to pay for two weeks' imports, India had no option but to open up its markets as it needed capital badly to pay for its essential imports like oil and gas. Multinationals saw this as their opportunity to target the sizable Indian middle class consumers.

As expected, Indian business owners began to feel the heat. For far too long they had become comfortable lording over their commercial fiefdoms in a protected economy. The threat of them losing their shirts to better products and services now looked like a real possibility. Their vocabulary didn't go past import control and the demand for a 'level playing field' – a euphemism for greater protection from cheaper and better imported products.

The patriot in CK could not bear to see India in such a hapless state from the comfort of his desk in Michigan. It pained him to see a country with a rich economic and cultural heritage and ample natural resources sliding into chaos and helplessness. He had to make a choice – of living his American dream, which he had worked very hard to earn, and ignoring the mess his country had gotten itself into or take a pledge to give his very best to make a substantial impact. The calling was too strong for him to resist.

CK was clear where he could leverage his strengths to contribute and areas to stay away from. This decision turbocharged him.

Despite living in the US since the mid 1970's, CK had his finger on the Indian pulse. He was perhaps one of the very few who instinctively believed in the resoluteness of the Indian spirit. He could do this because he was a keen student of Indian history – someone who looked for deeper meaning in India's many trysts with destiny. Above all, **he had an almost blind faith in the capacity of Indians as a race and as a culture to rise above their misfortunes.**

First things first, he told the group – that if they couldn't change how their country was run, they could at least begin by changing the way they thought and operated – an inside out rather than an outside in approach to transformation.

It was a time when most Indian businesses and its leaders suffered major credibility and trust deficits among the political and social communities. This prevented them from having a strong influence on policy and governance. CK wanted business leaders to be the change they wanted to see in the system, inspired by Mahatma Gandhi's most famous and influential quote ' *You must be the change you wish to see in the world.* '

Yet, CK did not want the leaders to think that he had a magic wand. He told them that he could make far more money during the three days he spent with them consulting, but he also made it clear that he was there for a purpose - to initiate a new direction and to unleash their latent potential. Anand Mahindra says: *"He was very much like a teacher who was there not for personal gain. Moral credibility and legitimacy gave him a podium to tell us why we should be listening to him."*

CEOs could connect with him instantly because he did not have a condescending attitude about their ability to change. He had respect for managers, a rare attribute among the academia. He had a taste of the corporate world during his early years working for Union Carbide and India Piston.

CK told them that he was not there to preach. He was there only to initiate new ways of looking at challenges and opportunities. Having been a teacher of strategy and a consultant for several blue chip American and European companies for more than a decade, he had deep insights into how multinational corporations functioned. He knew what they were good at and what they were not good at, inside out. He knew this was his trump card which he was willing to offer and business owners were eager to lap it up.

Was CK provocative enough to stir the dormant pride of Indian business leaders who had been weighed down by a potpourri of socialism and capitalism for six decades? Was it the beginning of the end of self-doubt and the awakening of self-belief that Indian companies were no sitting ducks?

On the first day of the first session at Windsor Club, CK's first question was - who did the business leaders think their real enemy was? This question stumped everyone. They thought it was a trick question. Sensing their unease and with a poker face, CK Prahalad looked straight at them and said they were their own enemies and that they were exaggerating their fear of the unknown. He said: *"If we want to compete across the world and export, we have to learn to compete first at home."* That they had to start changing their mindset from saying: **"We cannot compete with MNCs in India to saying that we can not only compete in India but we can compete with them anywhere else in the world."**

This came like a bolt from the blue to some and some thought the professor had probably lost touch with the Indian reality. CK kept his focus. But the situation was so dire, and the professor had flown from across continents to be there, that they were willing to test their own patience.

By the end of three days, truth began to dawn as the leaders started to see the merit in what the somewhat tall professor in his early 50s, sporting extra-large frame spectacles was saying. He told them that they could not fight using the same weapons that their enemy, many times bigger than them, were using. They had no choice but to radically reinvent themselves if they wanted to put up a good fight. He told them stories from history where smarter, smaller forces had fought the big successfully.

Krishna Kumar, one of Tata Group's most accomplished CEOs, who retired in 2013 along with Ratan Tata, went up to CK during the coffee break on the first day at Windsor Club session and told him how impressed he was with his presentation. CK didn't look very pleased which made KK wonder if he had said anything wrong. With a straight face, CK reminded KK of the tough times he had given him as his senior during the National Cadet Corps (NCC) parades in Loyola College, Chennai. This was an ice breaker.

CK and KK went on to enjoy one of the most cordial and professional relationships for almost two decades. It took CK closer to the 146-year old Tata Group. Many CEOs in the group companies say they were inspired by CK while the group metamorphosed from a large, trusted Indian business house, to a 100-company, $100-billion revenue global behemoth in 2013.

CK described his early days at CEO forum sessions as 'gut wrenching' and the more debilitating the disease, the harsher had to be the bitterness of the medicine.

The treatment seems to have worked. In two decades, almost all the business leaders who were there at the forum are not only India's stars in their domains in the domestic market but have a respectable presence in the global markets as well. That this metamorphosis happened in front of CK's eyes in just over a decade of his 'India Mission' must have given him a big high. He must have been ecstatic when Indian companies started acquiring marquee global brands like Jaguar Land Rover, Tetley, Novelis and many others.

The Windsor Club and the CEO Forums that followed were literally CK's lab for trying out his blue-print for transforming self-seeking Indian business leaders into nation builders. And making them think like global business leaders because he believed they could.

KV Kamath, the most regular of the lot at all the CEO forums, was eloquent at CK's memorial at Loyola College when he said: *"When you imagine India in the first ten years of liberalization, unable to compete, a morose capital market, here was CK telling us what was wrong. We heard him. But when he threw a googly* (a popular cricketing term for a kind of spin bowling that confuses batsmen) *that to compete in the global scale you have to be multinationals yourselves we were quietly laughing at ourselves. Lo and behold, ten years later in 2004, Indian investments going out were larger than foreign investments coming in."*

"He laid a very strong foundation of very hard work. You need to work hard to get where you are, you need to get your data, and analysis right and then you need to be able to connect the dots which is probably not visible to everyone. I think that is what distinguished CK from several other teachers I learnt from. To me the annual three-day forum was like a rejuvenation exercise."

CK told KV Kamath to see explore the opportunity of what technology could do to banking in India. In 1996 there were less than 100 ATMs in India. He said: *"You have to think big. If you need to bridge this gap between aspirations and resources, and I know that you have aspirations but resources are limited, you have to disrupt, you have to think of something completely different. He was egging me on all the time."*

CK got the CEO of NCR Corp. where he was a director, to India. A year and a half later ICICI Bank rolled out 1000 ATMs in one year. This feat seemed like a miracle because reliability of telephone lines then was not even 30 percent. CK asked Mr. Kamath to change the game and use satellite instead. Kamath agreed and the reliability of transactions went up to 90 percent.

"When you look back at these things, you think how was he able to make these connections? These connections are read by looking at where is

technology likely to head, where is India likely to head, what will the common man ask and how do you disrupt existing businesses and use technology as a lever," Mr. Kamath said.

Simple Questions, Difficult Answers

The debates during the first two years of the Windsor Club were on expected lines – cribs about too many rules, debilitating controls, highly restricted access to bank capital, a weak stock market, dilapidated infrastructure, huge trust deficit between politicians, bureaucrats and businessmen, high transaction costs and the governments' macro and micro economic mismanagement.

It's funny how one hears about these frustrations even in 2014, yet almost all the top Indian business groups, who participated in CEO forums regularly for 15 years, have emerged as India's most admired and envied today!

What magic did CK do which led this group of business leaders to re-imagine their future and go after it? What importance would business historians give to a teacher, coach, mentor and a friend of a good number of Indian business leaders when they write the post 1991 chapter of India's business history?

"I started with simple questions, but they were very difficult questions for companies," CK said in one of his talks. His questions were: *"Can established firms innovate? Can a company with a 100-year history innovate from within? Can they re-invent themselves? Should it always be an outsider who reinvents an industry? Can we create world class products in developing countries like India? Can India move to next practices?"*

CK didn't like Indian companies spending too much time benchmarking with global best practices. He asked them a pointed question: ***"Think conceptually what happens? If everybody is benchmarking everybody else, we gravitate towards mediocrity in a hurry. So I am much more focussed on next practices, not best practices."***

Such hard-hitting questions made CK very unpopular at first, but adored later. As the CEO forums rolled by, he became a magnet. In the later CEO forums, business owners brought their children, their CEOs and CXOs with them to listen to CK so that they could get back, prepare a blueprint for change and own the outcome.

It looked like CK had a premonition of the catalyst role he would be playing in transforming Indian businesses in the early 1970s itself. Every new place he went and every research paper he read, every company he consulted with, the question on the top of his mind always was – what can India learn from them?

CK's trip to Japan in 1972, as an MBA student at the Harvard Business School, may well have been the beginning of a long journey of wonder – reflection – learning – vision of a new India. CK saw emerging Japanese MNCs as prototypes for Indian companies. On his return, he would tell his family how he was thoroughly impressed by Japanese discipline, the intent they had to become global players, and the hunger to build scale. How it was the only way to provide jobs in a country that was teeming with population, unemployment and unemployability.

South Korea was another of CK's favourite examples. He would say that the Koreans had come from nowhere and look at the MNCs they are building? Referring to Samsung, LG and Hyundai, he told Indian leaders – *"You have no hope of surviving unless you focus,"* referring to his pet term, **'Core Competence'**.

Even when economist John Kenneth Galbraith called India 'a functioning anarchy,' CK believed in the ability of Indians to excel when they found themselves in crisis situations. He often referred to the Green Revolution, the manufacturing of super computers when the US denied access to key technologies in the 80's, success in missile and satellite launch technology, and the quick solution to the massive Satyam Computers scandal to make his point.

*"**Wherever we have failed it has always been a failure of leadership and because we didn't trust one another enough. But every time we have had clarity of thought, and true effort behind its execution, India showed it can deliver.**"*

CK didn't believe in telling CEOs what they should do, rather he made them believe that they could do it. He would tell business leaders that if they showed focus and a clear strategy, their organizations would support them. He said: ***"In the absence of vision and hope and belief, everything would descend into some form of zero-sum mentality."***

Adi Godrej, Chairman of the Godrej Group, also a regular at CEO forums, says: *"We got an impression that CK was talking about things that were not going to be very relevant for India. But within a couple of years we realized that it became extremely relevant, that elicited a great deal of interest among us to hear him. When he talked about good corporate governance, innovation and such esoteric topics, at first, one thought, it was way into the future, but soon we were convinced that CK was able to predict things very well.* **He was very practical in his approach, even though he was academically brilliant.** *The most important thing was – he was very passionate about India's success and India's progress, which we could see clearly."*

Godrej took his daughter Tanya Dubash along for two CEO sessions. She now manages the branding of the group which has grown to $4.1 billion in revenues in 2013 from a few hundred million in the 1990s. The company has been engaging faculty from the Ross School, whose brief is largely to professionalize the family-run company. Started in 1897, and operating in sectors as diverse as real estate, consumer products, industrial engineering, appliances, furniture, security and agricultural products, the real growth of the group was in the last decade. Godrej today has a presence in 60 countries and its overseas operations constitute 26 percent of its revenues.

Even You Didn't Know Why You Succeeded

In six years, between 1994 and 1999, CK made a tremendous impact on the psyche of Indian business leaders and senior executives and had influenced how they articulated their robust framework of how they would go about competing in difficult markets. The Tatas, Godrej, TVS, Murugappa Group, Wipro, HCL, the Jindals, ICICI Bank and hundreds of medium and small enterprises were raring to go. Public forums, especially the Confederation of the Indian Industry (CII) and Federation of Indian Chambers of Commerce and Industry (FICCI), Association of Chambers of Commerce (ASSOCHAM), National

Association of Computer Companies (NASSCOM) and others were energized to lobby for pro-industry reforms. CK spoke in all these forums regularly to packed audiences. He also used video-conferencing during CII's manufacturing conferences in Mumbai to reach out to thousands of small business owners across India.

Anand Mahindra, a Harvard alumnus, was one of the most active participants in the CEO forums. *"It was fairly a heady environment in which to interact and participate because just the quality of the minds around the table was very stimulating. CK was completely un-intimidated by this group of businessmen around him. He would constantly pummel us with the concept of focus. He was very concerned that Indian businesses were all over the place and would never be able to achieve excellence, let alone global scale unless they focussed on one thing and decided to do it better. He gave very little chance to any Indian business to survive without focus."* He believed that his theory of 'Core Competence' applied perfectly to India.

Like most other Indian business groups, M&M too thought CK's Core Competence theory was impractical in India. This theory demanded sharp focus on just one or two products or services. In a controlled economy with heavy shades of crony capitalism, leaders argued, everyone wanted a pie of a new business that presented itself as the economy was opening up after the 1991 liberalization. The size of the Indian middle class was turning out to be a juicy chunk as well which no Indian business could resist.

Michael Porter is the closest to what Anand Mahindra had as a guru until CK came along. Mahindra finds Porter's theories to be robust and practical. *"He is the only person I will describe as somebody whose management percepts I have followed."* Mahindra said: *"I was incorporating the concept of focus in a different way and I was doing it by creating independently listed companies. In a sense, the group had become like a private equity group. That was the way I incorporated the idea of focus but without losing the chance to build new businesses."*

Mr. Mahindra and his CFO Bharat Joshi soon become CK's good friends even if they didn't subscribe to his big idea then. *"We had a very personal and fond relationship as well."* They caught up between sessions and even had dinner at CK's home in San Diego. One dinner was truly special. CK told them while drawing a diagram on a piece of paper, which Anand Mahindra has preserved, that he was watching what they were doing with their auto business; that he was intrigued at how M&M had a rural network through their tractor business, and a finance business to finance it. *"What you are really doing is building 'Fortress Mahindra,' a unique ecosystem in your mobility area that is very difficult to penetrate."* Mr. Mahindra recollects: *"Bharat and I both vividly remember that, and I often use the phrase 'Fortress Mahindra,' when I talk to my analysts about the concept of 'an ecosystem in mobility'. That idea has endured."* By 2005, M&M, like several Indian business groups whom CK inspired, was galloping at a brisk pace.

Despite their bonding, Anand Mahindra was wary of CK's blunt ways of speaking his mind out not bothering if it was politically correct or whether it would hamper his consulting opportunity. Yet he couldn't think of anyone better to keynote his global conference in Goa in 2006 at the Mahindra Holiday resort.

Minutes before the start of the event, with a grin on his face, CK asked his host: *"Are you trying to tell me that you made it?"* He paused, and asked Anand Mahindra what he wanted him to speak about. Anand Mahindra was quite prepared for CK to *"...come in and launch a grenade into the tent and say this isn't working out. I was expecting him to launch a device and blast to smithereens everything we were doing. This conference was meant to be about new thinking, I was prepared for that."* But CK disappointed him.

Anand Mahindra remembers CK's words: *"I will be honest; I have begun to understand what you are doing. You have succeeded and I will give you credit for that."* He was taken aback. *"It was a big moment for me for CK to come up, after all these years of being slapped by him, to say you have succeeded."* He was blown away when CK chided him saying; *"I think even you don't know why you have succeeded."* Mr. Mahindra said: *"It turned out to be that the guru was patting his 'shishya' (disciple) on the back. That was to me the defining moment of our relationship with him."* The next minute CK was on the stage facing 500 people.

CK had done his research. On the Y axis he listed all the companies in the M&M group and on the X axis he listed out its competence - scale manufacturing, rural distribution, brand building, logistics, IT and telemetric. He had made a grid and populated it with the competence each sector had. It turned out that many sectors had overlapping competencies. *"CK stepped back and paused for dramatic effect. When he saw the effect was muted, he explained that if you really want to leverage what you have created it should not be that each sector does its own strategy independently. You will really leverage this if you look at the competencies that run across and then use all those competencies to enhance those businesses."*

After hearing CK in Goa, Anand Mahindra felt that CK's theory of Core Competence could easily have been misunderstood to mean that, simply by focussing on doing one thing well, you are going to succeed. *"That's why I think the Core Competence theory has become more like a buzz word, more like a conversational word. 'What's your core competence' has become a figure of speech."* Later, Anand Mahindra realized that CK's Core Competence was actually closer to Porter's concept of 'The Web' – a complex mechanism of competencies which are interlinked, which make it very difficult for competitors to enter.

Just like its peers the Mahindra group has galloped from a few hundred million dollar revenues a decade ago to revenues of $16 billion in 2013. It is today a global entity with operations in 100 countries; it is one of the top three tractor manufacturers in the world and has made some very smart acquisitions of global auto brands such as American Navistar and South Korea's Ssangyong in the last three years. It has set an audacious target of becoming the top 50 global brands by 2020. It's audacious because it's not even in the top 500 in 2014.

Wisdom in a Necklace

Every year at the CEO Forum CK would introduce a new theme and would delve deep into it after a recap of the previous years' themes. This approach, many leaders believe, differentiated CK from all other gurus they had heard. Others typically are superb at one concept but CK was able to see a broad panoply - how various elements hung together; how all this would lead you into entering new markets – type of discussions. **Ashok Soota says:** *"In a way, CK was looking at everything from the perspective of the CEO at all times."* Azim Premji, Chairman of Wipro, had pulled Mr. Soota and his CTO, Dr. Sridhar Mitta along to the Windsor Club sessions because they ran the IT business at Wipro. Soota built Wipro's IT business from scratch until the late 1990s. He went on to co-found Mindtree Ltd along with his Wipro colleague Subroto Bagchi.

Business leaders don't like anyone thrusting their ideas however bad their state of affairs could be. CK was conscious of this ego play and would say, as Ashok Soota remembers: *"This is your food for thought"* and would leave it at that. He wouldn't say 'go and conquer the world and become a star'. He'd say that the better way to challenge the dominance of MNC brands is first to find their own niche in the larger game, and focus on becoming a leader in it. Over a period this niche would become big enough to challenge MNCs in their own game. Wipro grabbed this advice and entered the 'lab-on-hire' segment of outsourcing around 1995-96. This is now a few billion dollar business.

Mr. Soota still remembers five or six major lessons from the more than 50 or so 'pearls of wisdom' he gathered from CK during the sessions. He remembers a popular line of Dr. Sridhar Mitta, Wipro's first Chief Technology Officer: *"CK's pearls of wisdom bind together nicely like in a necklace."*

Either at the CEO forums or in consulting, CK did not come across as someone who said he knew everything. **He would make it a point to say that he learnt from business leaders all the time.** His ingenuity was in extrapolating various factors in front of him through deep understanding of how they worked and articulating them lucidly so that business leaders could see a bigger picture. Soota says: *"He made business leaders think big, unsettled them from their comfort zone and rediscovered their own possibilities."*

CK had agreed to consult with Wipro on its global exploration mission after he managed to convince Dr. Mitta, that he and his company had the potential to play a bigger game than they thought they were capable of. Dr. Mitta remembers this dialogue with CK, which he thinks, was a defining moment for him and for Wipro.

Dr. Mitta recalls the early years when Wipro was trying to find its feet in the information technology sector. *"The basic questions on our minds were – how do you sell intellectual property; how do you evaluate which product or service create value to the customer; how do you sell value; how do you measure it? We didn't know anything when we started off. Our big sounding board was CK.* **He was the bridge between the global customer needs and Indian potential for creating them.** *When we were groping in the dark; CK shed light on a lot of things."*

Sometime in early 2000 when Dr. Mitta asked CK which global company Wipro should choose as a role model, hinting at the $20 billion Unisys, he didn't expect CK to tell him, with a half smile and a half smirk, that he shouldn't be following anyone. Instead, CK said: *"You become the Unisys."* Dr. Mitta thought CK was joking. He recalls: *"He never said anything to please you; he had confidence in me and Wipro that we could do it. That's how he was till he died. He made business leaders think big, imagine the impossible and chase it as if it was no big deal."*

In the next five years post this exchange, Wipro became one of the leading product development outsourcing companies in the world. Focus on global delivery of R&D services, instead of the lesser-skilled back office, manpower-intense operations of its peers like Infosys and TCS, placed Wipro in a different league. Wipro has maintained that identity even today making it less vulnerable to the whims of the American and European markets. Outside Wipro, Dr. Mitta and CK worked together in building 'The Indus Venture' popularly known as TiE, first in the US and later in India to create a community of entrepreneurs.

A few business groups were content with reading CK's books for inspiration. A senior Reliance Industries executive said the company's top executives were given a copy of the *'Fortune at the Bottom of the Pyramid'* article to explore products for the mass market. Unconfirmed anecdotes suggest Reliance's first mobile phones for the mass market in 2004-05, that sparked the telecom revolution in India, were inspired by the BoP business model. CK was a member of the Reliance Innovation Council formed led by top scientist Dr. RA Mashelkar.

A Tale of Three Women Bankers

The annual CEO Forum sessions in Mumbai from 2000 to 2009 were less animated compared to the sessions at the Windsor Club. The profile of the participants also was different –more CEOs and senior executives unlike earlier when more business owners showed up. CK started involving his Ross School of Business faculty more often and turned these sojourns into intense executive education classes as organizations needed senior executives to execute the grand strategies their business leaders had chalked out.

Regulars and those who have had a peek into one or two CEO forums were top management teams from Nicholas Piramal, State Bank of India, Marico Limited, Bharat Forge, Bajaj Electricals, Asian Paints, ITC Ltd, RPG Enterprises, Airtel and many more. The rich list shows how eager executives were for stimulus and drive.

ICICI Bank sent its entire senior management team to these forums regularly. The bank's senior leadership included its star trio Chanda Kochhar, Kalpana Morparia and Shikha Sharma. Under Mr. Kamath's leadership and CK's mentorship, they have turned out as one of India's most self-assured and dynamic teams. Yet the pressure of quarterly reporting was new to them and they hated it. They even had coined a term that explained how much they despised it –'QSQT'- an abbreviation of Bollywood star Aamir Khan's super hit debut film *'Qayamat se Qayamat Thak'* in the late1980s. Their version of QSQT was - *Quarter se Quarter Thak* (from quarter to quarter).

Kalpana Morparia says: *"We were all so bogged down with quarterly earnings so we coined this term."* She asked CK how she could live with such a monster. CK heard her out patiently and tried to show her various ways of managing expectations without losing perspective in terms of how we treat our business differently; how you could charge your people differently; how you create a market where nothing existed; how you could actually participate in the purpose of your company by actively collaborating with a number of players. *"He opened several windows to our mind. I think that's the greatest thing I learnt."*

Ms. Morparia joined J P Morgan Chase as CEO of South Asia and India Operations in 2009 after holding leadership roles at ICICI Bank for many years. She said she didn't feel she had missed CK's earlier sessions because CK had a deft way of bringing his audience up to speed with a quick encapsulation of the past along with detailing the challenges of the present and expectations of the future. She says: *"Even in 2005, he began with what the key theme was in 2000 and it gave you a fantastic perspective on how much the thinking had evolved in the country from saying – 'we don't want global MNCs competing here before we have a level-playing field – to a thinking that we want to create Indian MNCs."*

KV Kamath groomed Kalpana Morparia, Chanda Kochhar and Shikha Sharma to run ICICI Bank. The three have since grown wings. They head top banks and the media calls them the leading ladies of the Indian banking industry. Chanda Kochhar runs ICICI Bank as CEO while Morparia moved to lead J P Morgan Chase. Sharma joined Axis Bank as CEO, one of India's leading banks with a public sector heritage. In a way, CK's influence has spread to the Indian banking sector as well.

Ms. Morparia says: *"What influenced me at an individual level is the ability to say that you have to let go of your proven concepts and think differently. He would take us through flights of imagination. In my life, I have always been a very solutions driven person. I can find solutions to almost every problem that exists in the world but I was never very good at putting a conceptual framework around what I thought was the problem and the way we can look at it in a conceptual framework. CK helped me to do that."*

One of the reasons for ICICI Bank's phenomenal rise is attributed to how its senior executives think and act like entrepreneurs. She adds: *"CK used to push us to think like entrepreneurs and told us that we were lucky to have the luxury of an institutional framework that takes care of all the knitting so that you are not hampered by the typical administrative, financial and capital needs that an entrepreneur worries a lot about."*

She thinks everything that CK said definitely made sense to India Inc. as it was going through the pains of a completely different environment from a highly regulated to a market-facing economy. *"While we were riding that journey, he would give us a perspective of how things have changed through the years. **While we were so much engulfed by gloom that everything appeared like a big challenge, he had the ability to pull you out of that and show you what lies ahead."***

After joining J P Morgan Chase, Ms. Morparia went back to CK's CEO forum classes in 2009, she learnt even more from CK. She says: *"I thought how relevant CK can be in actually provoking thoughts among Fortune 500 companies. A lot of them had reached a dangerous stage of letting bureaucracies manage the complexity of global organizations. They are so much in love with their own world view of how things were going and were not challenging themselves enough."* She lists a dozen blue-chip giants, some of them her clients, which faltered big time in the 2008 recession. ***"They could have been saved if they had listened to CK."***

ICICI Bank and J P Morgan Chase are two different entities and cultures. Reflecting on how she could bank on CK to cope with her new job, Ms.Morparia says: *"The entire thing that was inculcated in us in ICICI is to say that to find a solution, you just need the ability to be very focussed on what it is that you have to do, have clarity of purpose and follow that, and execute that with unwavering intensity and focus. I think that has held me in good stead here. At ICICI I learnt to work as a team which is helping me a lot. J P Morgan is a matrix organization structure, so all the interpersonal skills that ICICI literally forced us to learn in an environment where we had to collaborate and work together, is another thing that is really helping me here."*

Yet Ms. Morparia believes CK could have left a more lasting impact if he had gone a step ahead with his 'Fortune at the Bottom of the Pyramid' concept by providing a framework and had set up a team to run a large fund that invested in BoP start-ups. She feels **it is high time consultants and gurus** *"had a skin in the game"* so that their ideas are tested out before they go main stream.

ICICI Bank CEO Chanda Kochhar also attended the Bombay CEO Forum for four years in a row between 2006 and 2009. She says:

"CK helped us to create in each of our own minds a fresh framework to think about value drivers and about how one could innovate to create value." Her more powerful learning, she says, was her sharp understanding about resources and value. ICICI Bank pioneered several concepts in Indian banking including micro insurance and insurance for diabetics. ***"ICICI's and CK's thoughts clearly overlapped on business opportunity in the mass market."***

Nachiket Mor was another senior executive in ICICI Bank who had turned CK's fan. He ran the ICICI Foundation for Inclusive Growth. CK convinced Mr. Mor that entrepreneurship at the grassroots level was a better way of addressing India's abject poverty conditions than through projects. Today, he is one of the most vocal leaders in India for taking healthcare into the mainstream of economic debate and investment. India's ranking on health care access is one of the worst in the world which Mr. Mor believes is an opportunity for the private sector to address using the BoP model in smaller towns.

He co-founded the IKP Trust in 2009, a non-profit that launched *SughaVazhvu* (means happy life in Tamil), the rural healthcare project in Tamil Nadu. It's an experiment in managed care –with a few trained health practitioners, electronic medical records and simple diagnostic devices. Eventually, the project aims to closely track and meet the healthcare needs of about 50,000 families for $40 a year.

Tata Nano

When Tata Nano was launched in 2009, the Tatas didn't have to spend a cent to advertise it. Generous global publicity poured for everything it represented, more for being the world's cheapest car than for its snazzy design, latest technology and innovative product and supply chain management. It's funny that Tata Nano desperately needed aggressive advertising in 2013 to push sales because the marketing department had goofed up right from the beginning by positioning Nano on price rather than on value. Tata Motors didn't get its first car, the Tata Indica, right the first time either.

Was Nano Mr. Ratan Tata's brainchild entirely? To what extent did CK influence his thinking? This is a delicate question in Bombay House, the Tata headquarters. People who saw CK's presentations, around 2004-05, remember a big picture of parents and three kids jostling for space on a scooter as the ideal target market for a small car and believe the Tatas could have picked it up from there. The Tatas, including Mr. Ratan Tata, insist it was their brainchild and it was sheer co-incidence that CK spoke about it as well.

True to CK's credo, the whole concept, Tata Nano's design to delivery began on a clean slate. CK would insist that radical ideas can succeed only if the whole process began on a clean slate. Incremental approach is the biggest enemy of innovators.

Ratan Tata says: *"He (CK) has been someone I have admired because he opened everybody's eyes to this huge base of the pyramid which most of us had seemed to ignore."* Yet, he thought CK fell short by not anticipating how the concept of 'pride of ownership' would play out with BoP products. *"My own experience with that segment of the market has been somewhat disappointing because what has also been evident, which I don't think Prahalad addressed, is a **sense of pride** of not being seen to be at the base of the pyramid. It amazes me how high value items are sold (bought) even at great distress but they (customers) will not take the items that are designed for them. This is because that would look as though they were buying it since they couldn't afford a better one."*

Perhaps CK didn't have the luxury of testing this nuance out because he died in April 2010, two years or so before the Tatas realized their gaffe. Ratan Tata rues: ***"I wish he and I had interacted more when we were doing the car project."***

What price will Nano pay for its marketing team's blunder, only time will tell. Mr. Tata says: *"Nano suffered greatly from that perception mainly because Tata Motors chose the soft option of saying it's the cheapest car rather than it's the best value car. I think we did that to ourselves."* The Tatas finally decided to re-launch the car as an aspirational smart city car for youth in 2014.

It appears CK's influence was most pervasive on the Tata Group. CK was virtually Ratan Tata's A team's chief coach, mentor, friend and *chief provocateur*. They had huge admiration and mutual respect for each other's professional acumen and ethical business practice. That many of the Tata companies' senior leadership came from Chennai or Coimbatore, where CK too grew up, helped in the smooth flow of single malt, Tamil and '*rasam*' (hot pepper soup) after a hard day's work.

The Tata – CK romance started when CK caught the Tata's attention when he estimated India's market size at 600 million, larger than that of China; which made him wonder why Indian business houses were making such a big fuss about threat from foreign competition. There was enough for everyone if right products at right prices were offered in the domestic market itself.

Ratan Tata said he was highly inspired by this view. He remembers another of CK's statements that got him thinking - *"The world is your market, why limit your imagination only to India?"*

Mr. Tata insists he was one of the few who welcomed foreign competition at all times and was not a party to the Bombay Club's demands for a levelplaying field. He said: *"I always felt that the Indian customer needed to have the chance to choose consumer products, automobiles, living accommodation etc. And that only competition would drive industry. There was a great deal of opposition for letting that happen because people wanted to continue protectionism."*

It's interesting that the timing of the CEO Forums in Mumbai from 2000 to 2009 and the Tata group's aggressive global acquisitions were around the same period. In a way, the Forum inspired many Tata senior executives to stay on the path of massive global expansion. The forum acted like a 'school for thinking and acting big' on the back of which Chairman Ratan Tata launched what seemed like outrageously ambitious global acquisition plans – Tetley in 2000, Daewoo Motors' commercial vehicle business in 2004, Corus Steel in 2006 and Jaguar Land Rover in 2008. These were among the 35 or so global acquisitions the Tatas made since 2000. It's quite likely that Tata senior executives' network with CK made it easier for them to translate Ratan Tata's vision into action on the ground.

It's interesting that between 1991 and 2013, the Tata group metamorphosed from an Indian conglomerate to a highly respected global entity. Its 100 or so companies generated revenue in excess of $100 billion in 2013 and had a market capitalization of close to 100 billion in September 2013. Ratan Tata regularly gets ranked as the most respected business leader in India by almost all surveys run by newspapers and magazines for nearly a decade.

Ratan Tata said he was *"...very impressed by the perspective and the statesmanship CK brought into the meetings and how he pushed the thinking one way or the other without imposing his viewpoint and setting milestones and gate posts along the way."*

To a question on the influence of management consultants or gurus on the Tatas, Mr. Tata said management consultants by and large focus on structures. *"Prahalad was different; he focussed on widening your imagination, in fact, in achieving certain things that were not in the box. And he encouraged thinking out of the box. Anybody could argue with me that most management consultants want you to go into the box, their box.* ***I think Prahalad opened your eyes by saying that it's not the box that counts, but your ingenuity, your innovativeness. I would say that he fostered innovativeness and you can't put that in a box, you can't create a code for innovation, it has to be the environment that you create and the openness of that environment. I think Prahalad succeeded in opening people's eyes to that."***

To those who followed Ratan Tata and CK it's evident that they were essentially dreamers and big risk takers. They dreamt of an India that took pride in its past and its ability to achieve its potential in the future – a country that could wipe out abject poverty.

But both have been sad with the way India has been governed in recent years. Mr. Tata doesn't hesitate to call India a 'banana republic' and doesn't mind *"getting chastised for it."* This is a real shame for an aspiring global super power especially because its most respected business person is saying it.

Tetley & Globalization

Tata Tea's acquisition of Tetley tea brand in 2000 could easily top the list of outrageously bold acquisitions by any company – the Indian company's net worth was one third that of the UK's top tea brand. It was also the first acquisition of a global brand by an Indian company. Harish Bhat's book *'Tata Log'* (Penguin India, 2012) captures the movie-like build up to the story, the anxious back-room discussions on how to raise such a huge debt. Finally,it was the pilot's adrenaline rush in Ratan Tata that sealed the deal.

The mammoth $440 million acquisition was the beginning of how Indian businesses shed their defeatist mindset and seeded a powerful thought that nothing was impossible if the intent was backed by strong purpose, a smarter ability to fund it and backed by daring leadership.

What Bhat's book perhaps missed is the crucial build-up of global aspiration among key Tata group CEOs, especially Tata Tea's CEO Krishna Kumar. It was CK's constant thrust in the 1990s that Indians should think global that lifted the veil that they had put on themselves. KK says: *"What does it take for Indian companies to globalize and the risks that you take and its opportunities were discussed extensively in CEO sessions. This really inspired me to make the first trans-border acquisition of Tetley."*

What's more, KK sought CK's guidance on integration of the two companies with disparate cultures. He notes: *"The purpose of an acquisition is to transform yourself before transforming them while you bring a new entity into the organization. That was the debate that I had with him several times. We went through practical problems on a wide variety of issues, be it marketing, HR management, and financial management. It was pretty intense."*

The Tetley experience showed that CK not only stood on the pulpit and preached; he also played a role in business transformation on the ground. He showed that he liked having his skin in the game, which he said he enjoyed thoroughly. Being hands-on came naturally to him, right from his days at Union Carbide when he was only 19.

The Tetley experience got CK and KK to go on a business opportunity hunting expedition. The Ginger Hotels project was their next big joint adventure. This project was pulled straight out of CK's Bottom of the Pyramid basket. During their many dinners together and while addressing business leaders, CK would discuss how hundreds of thousands of reasonably well-to-do pilgrims and their families had no decent facilities to sleep in pilgrimage towns across India. And business travel by small entrepreneurs was another big opportunity.

KK was then the head of India Hotels, the hotel wing of the Tata Group. After two years of hard work India's first smart-basic hotel called Ginger was launched in 2004 in Bangalore. It was inaugurated by Ratan Tata and CK was seen acting almost like its chief operating officer trying to see everything was perfect.

At $25 a night, Ginger had more gizmos than many five-star hotels in Bangalore. This created a new wave in the Indian hospitality sector when the so-called budget hotel owners went on a spree to upgrade theirs. With close to 50 properties in 2013, Ginger has been winning all the awards in its segment. In 2013 Lonely Planet called Ginger the 'best value hotel'.

By 2004, CK and KK had become good friends. KK says: *"I would say he was truly an outstanding force in the last 20 years. It started with business then it spread into different areas…He made people rise above themselves. I can't think of any intellectual leader in the last 25 years who can actually match CK.* Every generation has great leaders but he remained an enduring figure. What's even more unique about CK is that he always went beyond business and saw it as an integrating force of a society. That I think is a very unique signature of the man."

The Manufacturing Bug

Even though management teaching and writing had kept CK very busy since he moved to the United States in the mid 1970s, his love for manufacturing had not faded. He was very comfortable in the company of engineers and entrepreneurs.

B Muthuraman was Tata Steel's Managing Director between 2001 and 2009 – a period when the company, the blue chip of the Tata Group, metamorphosed from a Jamshedpur-based century old Indian company to a global name in steel making. In 2008 it won the Deming Prize, the most coveted award for business excellence and total quality management in the world. It was the only company to win this prize outside Japan for a long time. The excellence it had to reach to win this award also made the company one of the lowest cost producers of steel in the world.

CK had huge respect for Muthuraman for turning Tata Steel into a globally competitive company despite operating in difficult Indian conditions. But Muthuraman says no one inspired him more than CK. *"CK's faith in Indian manufacturing was honey to my ears. A lot of us used to think, after looking at China, that India had no future in manufacturing. But CK made us think big. Because of him we started believing that manufacturing is not necessarily about repeatability, not only about scale. It is also about innovation."*

CK's enormous faith in the ability of an average Indian to innovate at an elementary level rubbed off on Muthuraman. Tata Steel's faith in its 35,000 people is what led them to go for the very harsh and process-driven Deming Award. He told Muthuraman that an **organization's potential can be unleashed only by creating a mindset of stretch and creating passion among ordinary people.** *"He had a terrific belief in the power of the ordinary worker."*

Muthuraman says CK made Tata Steel think of steel not as a commodity but as a service – a radical approach to how the value of a commodity is enhanced. This led to changes in the way steel was distributed. ***"CK put the thought in my mind that even steel can be differentiated by creating value for customers.*** *Since then, Tata Steel's distribution has been more like a retail fast moving consumer goods (FMCG) product than a business-to-business model. He kept telling us that steel can be a service."*

CK's engagement with the Tatas went beyond his engagement with Tata Tea, India Hotels or Tata Steel. He had taken on himself the mantle to make leaders out of every Tata executive. CK regularly spoke to hundreds of young Tata executives at the Tata training college in Pune. The high point of this relationship was when CK moderated a panel comprising three top Tata CEOs – Ravi Kant of Tata Motors, S Ramadorai, Vice Chairman of Tata Consultancy Service and Tata Steel's B Muthuraman at a Pan Indian Institute of Technology Summit in Chennai in 2008.

CK, along with Jamshyd Godrej, and Planning Commission member Arun Maira, former head of Boston Consulting, looked like they had taken the onus of making India a strong manufacturing power. The problems looked so daunting that no one even believed that it was possible. The trio ran several annual India manufacturing summits in Mumbai using the Confederation of Indian Industry platform.

Jamshyd Godrej says: *"All his interventions over the years were about internal change within organizations that would allow manufacturing to grow. He always focussed on the internal aspects within a company rather than issues to do with the country. He felt that the bigger issues about the country like infrastructure could not be individually addressed by companies but they could individually address their own comparative positions in the world. And despite all the constraints that existed, they could think differently so that they could emerge as globally relevant."* This galvanized hundreds of business leaders to launch a quality movement in India in the last two decades. It's interesting that India has the maximum number of ISO 9000 and other capability model certifications.

Muthuraman is certain India has a promising future in manufacturing because he believes that no country in the world with a sizable population has ever reached prosperity without going through a phase of manufacturing growth. It started with the United States, moved to Japan, then to China. India cannot escape it. A business friendly policy regime with an ambient entrepreneur eco-system is needed for this to happen. Despite knowing this fundamental truism, the Indian political establishment has been lax mainly because it viewed industry as a rich source of rent seeking rather than as a source of creating wealth and employment to fight poverty. Crony capitalism is no longer a dirty concept.

Manish Sabharwal, Chairman of staffing company Team Lease, who was on the skills development panel along with CK in the Planning Commission, remembers CK equating high unemployment and unemployability rates to that of a national security problem. *"He was the first to conceptualize that we don't live in an economy, we live in a society. If people don't have jobs you will have social problems and that is a much deeper problem than an economic problem."*

Manish has been a crusader for labour reforms in India but is disappointed at the lack of political will. He says that despite India becoming the fourth largest economy, it is also one of the poorest countries because 90 percent of its workforce is still in the informal sector. He says misplaced political priorities, obstructive laws and an unimaginative education system have ensured that the workforce indicators have remained the same since 1991 while all other indicators have moved up. Growth hasn't led to transformation of the labour market. *"Has India missed its tryst with destiny?"* he asks. Only progressive reforms, he believes, have the potential to boost India's stuttering growth since 2010.

Get on Your Own Feet

Microsoft was the only multinational IT company CK worked with in India. He was on its advisory board for three years when Ravi Venkatesan was Microsoft India chairman. Venkatesan was greatly influenced by CK's book on 'Core Competence' while he was doing his doctorate at Harvard Business School in the early 1980s. While in Microsoft (2004 - 2012), Venkatesan was itching to do something that had greater relevance to the society as he had had enough of corporate life. When he got some personal time with CK at a conference, he popped the question. CK told him, without a hint of patronizing, that it was high time he became like him - an entrepreneur, not necessarily starting a business, but going out, standing on your own legs and doing things that had a larger purpose. Venkatesan quit Microsoft in 2012 and founded Social Venture Partners India, whose purpose is to build a network of engaged leaders attempting to address complex social issues through venture philanthropy.

He thinks CK had a very strong marketing mind and a powerful way of packaging simple ideas. About the 'Fortune at BoP', it's not that nobody had said these things before, but he packaged them in an extraordinarily compelling way.

Venkatesan too shared CK's anguish during his last years about India stuttering with its reforms and governance standards. He used his earlier experience of running Cummins in India and later Microsoft

India, to vent his frustration in his book *'Conquering the Chaos: Win in India, Win Everywhere'*. The positive take away for MNCs from this book is that if they want sizable business growth in emerging markets, and other developing countries, they will have to cut their teeth in making their business work in India, however difficult it is. This is because all other markets are more or less in the same mould.

"I came to a very counter intuitive argument that India is so chaotic and hard that companies must strive to make it here because most emerging markets look exactly like this. They don't look like disciplined China, they look like chaotic India. Africa, most of South America, most South East Asian countries like Vietnam, all are just like us. And therefore companies can ill afford to ignore India."

In the last fifteen years or so, India had become a litmus test for MNCs in their efforts to succeed in other emerging markets. In the book, Venkatesan wonders how, in a similar chaotic environment, a good number of multinational companies like Unilever, P&G, Philips, Samsung, LG, Sony, Hyundai, and technology companies like IBM and GE have been able to do spectacularly well.

One of the biggest hurdles Indian subsidiaries of MNCs faced for so long was their top down approach. Their headquarters had little clue about how these markets functioned and were stubborn about treating them like their extensions. Companies in which CK was on board like Hindustan Lever (subsidiary of Unilever) had the benefit of CK's insight on India.

It's puzzling to see India continuing to treat the multinational companies shabbily even when they are beginning to contribute significantly to the growth and depth of Indian economy. CK was mortified to see this and was at a loss to explain to global CEOs other than asking them to be patient. Demand for retrospective tax on Vodafone in 2011 was a shocker. The flip flops on foreign direct investment in the retail sector also showed that politics and economics in India are rarely in sync with each other. Political expediency has crowded out all other rationale in public policy. Rigid labour policies have stunted growth in the manufacturing sector.

Says Venkatesan: *"All the governments take MNCs for granted. Every MNC, including Microsoft and IBM, is harassed, especially with regard*

A young CK Prahalad

Working the numbers at Union Carbide

Graduation Day at Harvard -- with wife Gayatri

At Pan IIT Dialogue with Tata Group CEOs - Ravi Kant (Tata Motors), B Muthuraman (Tata Steel) and S Ramadorai (TCS)

CK Prahalad with RBI Governor Raghuram Rajan (middle) and Tarun Das, CII Mentor

CK Prahalad, Gayatri Prahalad and Deepa Prahalad with US President, Bill Clinton

CK Prahalad with Gary Hamel (standing) and Peter Senge (middle)

Sharing a joke with Deepak Parekh of HDFC Bank

CK Prahalad and Al Gore, US Vice President

CK Prahalad, Amartya Sen (middle) and Suren Dutia,
President of TiE, San Diego

CK Prahalad with singer, Jon Bon Jovi

CK Prahalad with Indian Hotels CEO, Krishna Kumar

CK Prahalad with Indian Prime Minister Manmohan Singh

CK Prahalad with Jamshyd Godrej

CK Prahalad with Marshall Goldsmith

CK with members of Madras Management Association

to taxation issues. We never had any voice at the table. In the PM's advisory group there were only Indian companies. It's important to know that MNCs too bring a fair amount of income to the government."

CK heard out Ravi's anguish patiently. Instead of simply ranting, CK asked Venkatesan to organize a conference under the Confederation of Indian Industry exclusively for MNCs. Like a good student, he followed CK's advice and quickly put together a conference in which CK gave the opening keynote. This was only four months before he passed away. Now, MNCs at least have a forum to voice their concerns. India has not learnt from the experience of China, South Korea, Thailand and Malaysia as to how they took advantage of MNCs' superior operations and financial management skills.

There's hope that a new political dispensation after the 2014 general elections could perhaps initiate a new phase that is pro reform and pro governance. If these two are in place, usually economic and social development take care of themselves.

Simplifying Complexity

Manvinder Singh Banga, popularly known as Vindi Banga, was a top executive at Hindustan Lever when CK was on its board. He relives a scary incident. *"About 10-12 years ago I was a part of a group of senior Unilever managers who were called by the board in UK. Our brief was - can you guys think through what should be the vision, strategy and the direction of the company for the next 10 years? We were given two weeks to do this; CK was our leader, our facilitator. We spent 12 days unloading all our problems on each other, grievances on each other and on CK. We also produced thousands of recommendations in those 12 days.*

On the 12th night, some of us began to feel a little uneasy, we had only 36 hours to go before the entire board, and quite honestly, we hadn't a clue. I was the most worried because I had somehow been deputed as the presenter, so I was going to have to stand there and I didn't have a single chart ready. That's when CK took the stage and in three hours he somehow made us make all sorts of connections. He allowed us to get bothered and smothered in that complexity but from there we saw patterns and something emerged. At the end of three hours we had a vision, we could write in two lines and we had four clear action points and that was it. The rest is history because a lot of that impacted Unilever in the next 10 years."

Mr. Banga says **CK saw opportunities where many others saw problems.** *"I recollect one evening he walked into my home in Mumbai having spent the entire day in one of the world's largest slums, Dharavi. I thought he is going to come and tell me how terrible it was, how grim and dirty. He walked in with the same radiant smile we have seen in all his pictures and he told me what a great market potential and you are not exploiting it. So when others saw poverty, where others saw lack of hygiene, he actually came back with a different picture. He said there are multiple wage earners living in each room, they are not paying taxes and they have huge disposable income. Let's send our salesmen there."* Mr. Banga believes the seeds of CK's ground-breaking 'Bottom of the Pyramid' theory were sown here.

It's clear now that Hindustan Lever was CK's lab to test many of his hypotheses. After testing his BoP hypothesis, his next was that entrepreneurship was the cure to many social and economic problems in society. Mr. Banga says: *"He worked hand- in-hand with us to create something called Project Shakti. We worked with self-help groups to identify women who we could up-skill and create as distributors for our products deep into rural India. We would train otherwise illiterate women in 72 hours and equip them to become business women."*

In 2014, some 60,000 women entrepreneurs cover a population of a hundred million deep in rural India where there is poor road and media connectivity. These women doubled their household income in no time. Women started to gain social respectability and for Unilever it was competitive advantage in distribution. *"**What a tremendous win-win he helped us create.**"*

Hindustan Lever had gotten used to CK's unconventional ways. Yet, Banga was taken aback when CK persuaded him to invite the wives of the members attending the company's annual strategy conference. Mr. Banga remembers this episode well. *"We started the session. All the directors stood up and presented their individual business plans and then I handed the floor to CK. It's amazing how quickly he got all the wives into the discussion and within 10 minutes there were a couple of home truths on the table."* The wives were brutally honest. They said Unilever's product quality did not deserve the price premium. Executives got to see how bitter home truths really are.

No true Indian MNC yet

Jairam Varadaraj, MD, Elgi Equipments Ltd, known popularly as Jay, is one of the few business leaders who connected with CK both professionally and personally. He could fathom the depth of CK's intense engagement with India's transformation because he had followed his thoughts since his student days at the University of Michigan. CK was on the committee that decided to grant Jay his doctorate at Ross School of Business. He surprised CK with his thesis topic *'Why Indian Companies are not Competitive?'* which CK thought was a very bold choice then.

When Jay met CK ten years later at the CEO Forum, nothing much had changed except that the 1991 reforms had thrown up more doubts and fears than opportunities. Jay attended five of the CEO sessions.

Since both were from Coimbatore, Jay hit it off well personally with CK. He even helped CK locate his home in Coimbatore which CK felt like seeing after four decades. When they reached the place, close to a temple, an old man sprung out of a small house, stared at CK for a while, and in joy called out his childhood name, Billy. Jay was amused that CK, of all people, could have had such a nickname.

Jay is not as euphoric as many Indians are about the emergence of Indian global enterprises. *"Our typical tendency, even now, is to call a company an MNC if a big part of their business is from outside India. The actual definition of an MNC to me is being completely independent of any one country."*

Today, he says, several Indian companies have become international by building a portfolio of companies. *"Are they truly MNCs? No!...If, today, we are fed up with the way the government is handling the economy, do we have the competencies in the company and the organizational bandwidth to say, to hell with India, I am going to set up manufacturing and operations in a country that wants me the most? No one has that com-*

petence yet. We are still very India-dependent." He thinks most global facing Indian groups are not multinationals yet – they are simply a portfolio of companies.

After Jay came back from Michigan he started working in his compressor business but didn't achieve anything significant to be proud of. "*When these forums came along they became a very fertile ground for me to start refining my own thinking and sharpening my skills. That was purely CK, the aspiration was mine but the confidence, the instigation, the trigger and the kind of stimulus to think through came from CK.*"

Today Jay confidently claims: "*In manufacturing compressors, we have the 'know why' as good as the rest of the world. We can teach companies how to build and design compressors. Earlier, we were selling in Africa and the former USSR because customer standards were low. Today, half of our revenues are from outside, 60 percent are either from Europe or US. Today, we have subsidiaries manufacturing in China, Italy and France. We have our own companies in America, Brazil, Australia, Indonesia, and Thailand.*" When Jay started in the 1980s, his company's revenue was $15 million. Today, it is a respectable $250 million.

Jay says that despite major transformation of Indian business in the last two decades, CK's agenda is still not finished. He remembers CK saying -- Yes, you become more international, the technology is at par with the rest of the world, you have built brands, but the final point is – **Can you truly move anywhere in the world and no country can hold you hostage?** Jay thinks this is still a work in progress and for him "*…that continues to be the energizer, how do we build that? We still have a long way to go but that is the direction.*" This could be the direction all Indian companies would want to take.

Chapter 5

Global Impact --
Don of Business

He had this great gift to get people together, to show them a different way of thinking. What we had to do amounted to no less than a corporate cultural revolution of immense magnitude. **Jan Timmer, CEO, Philips, on reviving Philips during his tenure**

CK Prahalad's 'Fortune at the BoP' taught us to unlock the enormous potential. In fact, it was the root of the success of HUL, root of our success in many other places. The Unilever Sustainable Living Plan and the Standards of Corporate Behaviour we are setting up would not have been possible without him. **Paul Polman, Chairman, Unilever**

CK was loved by this board of directors. He was someone who the board counted on, his opinion mattered. He impacted the company by making sure that NCR didn't lose its focus on innovation. **Bill Nuti, Chairman, NCR Corporation**

It was a bright morning in July 1991 when CK dashed into a room full of waiting Royal Philips Electronics' top executives at their headquarters in Amsterdam. He looked grim. Without the usual pleasantries, he brandished a report from the local newspaper that morning, which said that Philips was headed towards bankruptcy and that the bankers wanted to know what the management's game plan was.

CK saw stunned faces. He paused for effect, but he didn't give them any time to vent their disbelief among themselves. They looked as if the ground was falling off under their feet.

Jan Timmer had just joined Philips as its new CEO, which he described as a moribund company needing an invasive surgery. Luckily for him, he had found a surgeon with whom he said he had a 'meeting of minds' during their first lunch meeting itself. Together, they were ready to launch Project Centurion – a long and painful exercise to revive Philips. It was called Centurion because it was exactly hundred years since the company was founded in 1891.

Timmer handed over the operation theatre to CK and was happy to play the role of his 'side kick'. CK was not new to Philips. He was already teaching there and knew what and where the malaise was. It's just that its senior executives were in royal denial which forced CK to use unconventional methods to force them to act.

Once the shock treatment was delivered, CK and Timmer called the 100 top executives to an auditorium, split them into two groups and gave them three hours and a one line brief – come back with a revival plan as if it is your last.

Timmer let CK take the centre stage while he hung around. He describes this day vividly: *"CK threatened them. He predicted doom and gloom and he held up the mirror to them and showed them how terribly bad they were. **He was like an exorcist, driving out all the bad habits of these people and he did that in very clear terms.** I have hardly ever seen him so hard and direct."*

After three hours, the two groups got back with a restructuring plan which surprisingly exceeded CK's expectation – a proposal to lay off 50,000 people, about 15 percent of the workforce. By then, the mood had turned from hostile to a can-do. *"This is one of the most memorable events to have happened in my professional life. It was all based on that meeting of the minds, on intuition, on an incredible understanding of each other's ideas,"* Timmer recollects.

Once the executives had come to accept the inevitable they opened up to a constructive dialogue. *"He was also a redeemer; he could show them the way forward. He could also make them believe in their strengths. He showed them how great a company Philips was,"* Timmer says. *"The session went uninterrupted from Thursday to Sunday with only a couple of hours of sleep a day."*

"He had this great gift to get people together, to show them a different way of thinking. What we had to do amounted to no less than a corporate cultural revolution of immense magnitude. I was sitting modestly along the side lines and we played the bad guy and good guy because, sometimes, he hit them too hard and I had to come in and make things a little nicer, and sometimes, it was the other way around."

Once the revival process was set to go, CK revealed that he had made up the news story because he wanted them to realize how serious the situation was. The executives must have cursed CK for pulling such a nasty one on them then, but would have been grateful later that he did that.

What made CK succeed? Remember he was a rank outsider – an American professor of Indian origin trying to teach hard-nosed Europeans what to do. How did 100 senior executives turn their scepticism into hope and trust? Timmer says: *"He triumphed not because of his extraordinary skills as a teacher or a provocateur, but they all felt he was a very fine human being. He was extraordinarily decent and he was very humble. He was a people's man and the audience sensed that and they went with him."*

Once there was buy in for the harsh restructuring game plan, Operation Centurion was spread over many years. *"Philips owes CK a great debt for all he did to us, we will never forget him,"* Timmer said during CK's memorial in Michigan. The two saved Philips from imminent bankruptcy.

CK had become every Dutch man's hero for saving thousands of jobs by reviving Philips. Many years later, a taxi driver, while trying to chat up his passenger, said he had heard of an Indian professor who had magically revived Philips, without knowing that he was talking to the same man.

Fritz Philips, grandson of the founder of Philips, visited CK's family at Ann Arbor in the mid-1990s to say how indebted he was to CK. He also shared how the Germans had occupied his home during the Second World War, but the army took care of them very well because they thought they didn't have to leave. He also said that a part of Karl Marx's *Das Kapital* was written in his home.

CK's hands-on experience in Union Carbide and India Pistons had given him the confidence to engage in conflict resolution by balancing the interests of both the people and the demands of business – a rare quality in a professor. Such experiences came in handy when CK taught senior executives during executive education programmes all over the world. Executives rated CK as one of the top teachers in polls by prominent business magazines in the US for more than two decades.

It was CK's firm belief that businesses should get the full value of the ideas of management teachers – if leaders didn't get value from his ideas, he was doing something wrong. He used consultancy as a way to learn about the issues CEOs really cared about. This approach took CK to work with the boards of very well- known companies such as NCR Corporation, Unilever India, Philips, Microsoft India and TVS Capital for a long time. For more than thirty years, CK consulted with blue chip enterprises such as Citibank, General Motors, Eastman Kodak, Pearson, P&G, Target, AT&T, Philip Morris, Oracle, Cargill, Honeywell, Motorola, Colgate-Palmolive, TRW, Whirlpool and Alstom.

It's not surprising that *Thinkers 50* listed CK twice consecutively in 2007 and 2009 (a once in two year ranking) as the world's number one most influential management thinker and advisor. This status was enjoyed only by Peter Drucker until then and in 2013, the honour was shared by innovation guru, Clayton Christensen as well.

What follows gives you a peek at a few companies, organizations and people CK influenced in different ways as a coach, mentor, strategist or simply as a sounding board for global CEOs. It's also an attempt to scan the world of thought leadership on strategy, innovation, entrepreneurship, sustainability and poverty – all of which CK influenced significantly for three decades and how he wanted everyone to appreciate their interconnectedness. And how he opened up whole new streams of intellectual enquiry and choices countries, companies, students and teachers could make if they anticipated and adopted what he called 'Next Practices' instead of trying to match best practices.

Professors can Impact Business

What made CK a global phenomenon? Why was he one of the most sought after keynote speakers in the last two decades in global conferences whose auditoriums were more than full all the time? Why did Fortune 500 companies vie with each other to have him on their board or consult for them? How significant is his idea of the 'Fortune at the Bottom of the Pyramid' to eradicate the curse of poverty from the planet? Did many companies survive and thrive because he showed them a new market to explore? To what extent did his principle of co-creation of value along with consumers contribute to the social media revolution? Will his prophecy that sustainability will drive innovation in the future save the world from imminent ecological catastrophe?

One could easily include a few more questions but the answers to all of them are beyond academic interest. They can even inspire usually cynical professors to actually believe that they too can make a big difference if they choose to. They could make 'know-all' executives believe that professors can indeed influence and impact business outcomes in a significant way.

CK was very choosy with whom he worked. His clients were either facing existential dilemmas or leadership blackouts. He also chose companies which had the potential to make a big impact and where the top management was open to fresh thinking. It appears he couldn't do much with Kodak, Motorola, AT&T and GM when they were struggling. The burden of their dominant logic was so strong that even CK could do little to alter their fate. However, those who were open to his ideas like Unilever, Philips, NCR, Pearson, Citibank, are flourishing and are testing new frontiers.

Everything seemed hunky dory for global MNCs until the world economic order began to shift in the last two decades. Not many had seen this coming. The markets in developed economies started to saturate from the early 1990s and MNC CEOs found themselves fighting for pieces of the same pie. Most of them had no clue how to expand into emerging markets and even if they did, how to minimize their risk. All emerging markets looked alike to them – poor governance, non-existent copyright protection, suspect market size and unskilled talent. It looked like they were more interested in keeping their jobs and bonuses rather than risk going after unchartered territories. The Enron saga had also scared them no end.

Jaithirth Rao (Jerry Rao) was one of Citibank's rising stars to take on global roles in early 1990s. That's when Citibank's Bill Campbell hired CK to consult for him.Citigroup's co-chief executive, John S Reed's choice to recruit Campbell to run the consumer business was somewhat controversial. Campbell was chairman of Philip Morris USA, but had no banking experience. But Reed stuck to his decision because he wanted people who could bring new thinking to the banking business. Since Citibank's audacious goal was to build a brand identity as big as that of Coca Cola, he betted on Campbell's vast marketing experience. Campbell spotting CK to drive the change in Citibank seemed logical because there were very few management professors with radical ideas and fewer who could deliver them as effectively as CK did.

Jerry said he attended several sessions CK conducted for senior leadership at the bank. *"This must have been the mid-90s when CK had not yet fully articulated his bottom of the pyramid (BoP) idea but he was working on it. It was quite clear because he was pushing us to mass market and not be an upscale bank."* CK got Citicorp leaders to relax when he told them that strategic planning was not rocket science. Jerry remembers CK saying: *"It doesn't require very complicated quantitative stuff. It only requires common sense, and requires stuff that we all agree upon as to what the future is going to be."*

In their classic HBR article (August 2003) titled 'The End of Corporate Imperialism', CK Prahalad and Kenneth Lieberthal wrote: *"Success in the emerging markets will surely change the shape of the modern multi-*

national as we know it today. For years, executives have assumed they could export their current business models around the globe. That assumption has to change. Citicorp, for example, aims to serve a billion banking customers by 2010."

You can Accomplish Anything

NCR Corp. called the 'self-service technology giant,' has been revolutionizing the way people connect, interact and transact with business for two decades. In 2008, TIME magazine's cover story, highlighted the global self-service movement as the number two revolutionary idea and identified its CEO Bill Nuti as the thought leader behind it.

"The best way to describe CK is, he's an out-of-the-box guy who is pragmatic," Hewlett-Packard CEO Mark V Hurd, who ran NCR Corp. (NCR) until March 2005 when Bill Nuti took over said. CK had joined the NCR Corp. board in 1997 and was active when he passed away in 2010.

When a company institutes an award in someone's name it is usually out of respect, gratitude, for significant contribution and also how much he or she is liked by the senior management. NCR Corp. gave its first 2011 **C K Prahalad Innovation Award** to Brian Connell, a software engineer, and Dave Norris, an engineering manager, for their work in the development of Scalable Deposit Module (SDM) technology. SDM is one of NCR's most recent ATM innovations and enables the simultaneous deposit of cash and cheques through a single slot, making the deposit process twice as fast unlike other ATMs.

Bill Nuti says: *"CK inspired us to move beyond what we believed to be possible – and use the power of innovation to change human behavior. We created this award to honor CK and his passionate focus on innovation. Brian and Dave's work on our SDM technology is the embodiment of the values Dr. Prahalad lived."* The award is bestowed annually to NCR employees for their development of 'disruptive innovation' that promises dramatic improvements in customer value.

This quote of Bill Nuti shows CK touched people's hearts as well as their minds. *"CK was loved by this board of directors. He was someone who the board counted on, his opinion mattered. He impacted the company by making sure that NCR didn't lose its focus on innovation."*

A long stint at the NCR Corp board gave CK and the company the opportunity to maximize each other's potential. *"CK had three-dimensional qualities – he was strategic, he could be operational, he could be someone who was inspirational and motivational as well. CK was fun to be around – caring and compassionate. CK was inspirational from the point-of-view that he believed in reaching well beyond the boundaries that we place on ourselves. He was someone who would feel very comfortable looking for the disruptive changes in technologies and quantum improvements in cost and quality. He would leave you believing you could accomplish anything."*

CK joined the NCR Corp. board at a time when it was spun off as a separate company by AT&T in 1996. Since then NCR has grown at a clipping pace with revenues in excess of $ 6 billion in 2013. It shows what strong leadership, an influential board with an avant-garde professor for inspiration, can achieve.

If India today accounts for 62 percent of NCR's overseas market, it's clear who had a hand in it. With only 80 ATMs per million in India against close to 1500 ATMs per million in developed markets, the growth opportunity is immense. But with mobile banking beginning to play a bigger role in India and other developing countries, NCR's innovation engine may have to tap into CK's 'Next Practices' mantras to stay relevant.

When Bill Nuti spun off Teradata in 2007, he ensured CK was on the board of that company as well. It shows how CK was part of the action all the time even in a very high tech environment. CK was at ease while talking about cutting edge technology trends such as cloud and big data at global conferences. He viewed these two as big drivers for bridging the digital divide between the West and the East. CK's daughter Deepa Prahalad says her father was very effective in bridging academics and business because he was constantly in touch with ground reality.

Unilever - BoP Lab

The day Paul Polman joined Unilever, the second biggest global consumer goods brand in 2009, he abolished sales and profit forecasts and quarterly guidance reporting. *"I did that the first day I became CEO because I simply figured that they can't fire me the day they hire me."* It was the beginning of a journey of transformation of Unilever from a stock market oriented consumer goods business to the one that declared its purpose in the ambitious 'Unilever Sustainable Living Plan' (USLP) in 2010.

USLP is Unilever's ambitious initiative to *"decouple our growth from our environmental impact, while at the same time increasing our positive social impact."* Its 2020 goal is to *"improve health and well-being, reduce environmental impact and source 100% of our agricultural raw materials sustainably and enhance the livelihoods of people across our value chain."*

Even before Paul Polman joined Unilever as CEO, the company had a management guru in CK on its board who was influencing the strategic direction of its global business since the late 1990s. Paul Polman and CK hit it off well especially when they had a chance to have a long chat on a plane on their way to Kenya's tea plantations.

Even before joining Unilever, Polman was keeping a close watch on how CK was redefining the fundamental construct of the FMCG (fast moving consumer goods) market in developing countries. During his acceptance speech of the '2012 CK Prahalad Sustainable Leadership' award from Corporate Eco Forum (www.corporateecoforum.com), he said: *"CK brought the concept of the BOP well into the company even before he wrote the book. We are grateful for what he has done for the company."*

Although CK was on the board of Unilever's Indian subsidiary, Hindustan Unilever for ten years, he had a clear influence on the company's global strategy. Polman observed: *"The USLP would not have been possible without CK because next to a business thinker, and an academic, **he was a friend of Unilever, a trusted advisor, and in some sense, a voice of conscience for us as we were developing our business model."***

The launch of USLP in November 2010 in New Delhi, six months after CK died, was the company's tribute to him. The company believes that the 'Fortune at the BoP' idea helped unlock its enormous potential. ***"In fact, it was the root of the success of HUL, root of our success in many other places,"*** Polman said.

More than all this, Polman says a seemingly simple replacement of the preposition 'of' with 'with' in its business strategy lexicon is making a world of difference to Unilever. He said: *"His mantra that was always striking to me from the first day was that we are not producing for the BOP but we are producing with the BOP. It's a small word difference but it makes a huge difference. With this, he brought dignity to people, people who felt they were nobody, he made them into somebody."*

Unilever's tryst with India began in the summer of 1888 when its crates full of Sunlight soap bars, embossed with the words 'Made in England by Lever Brothers' landed on the Kolkata harbour. Its brands *Lifebuoy, Pears, Vim, Ponds, Lipton Tea* and *Dalda* are household names in India and many parts of the world.

Just like physical scientists, economists and social scientists too need a lab to experiment their hypothesis before broadcasting their theories. At Unilever, CK could experiment his BOP concept much before the famous article 'Fortune at the Bottom of the Pyramid' was published in 2002. And when Unilever announced its USLP strategy in 2010, it resembled a perfect blend between CK's vision of sustainable communities using BOP products and services.

Unilever's *Project Shakti* helped CK to respond to his critics that BOP impoverishes people even more by making them spend on non-essentials. Instead, it showed that availability of affordable hygienic products enhanced the productivity of the consumers it served and also created thousands of micro entrepreneurs in villages. A community of entrepreneurs usually creates a culture of dynamism – badly needed to lift the spirits of people in the remote villages.

India – World's Innovation Hub

Inspired by CK, Citibank launched Citibank *Suvidha* (meaning convenience in Hindi) as a pilot project in Bangalore in 1997. It was designed especially for salaried individuals with features such as utility bill payments, automatic creation of fixed deposits, direct credit of salary reimbursement, among others. Seeing its instant success, many banks started to offer these facilities. People who were frustrated with long queues even for simple banking transactions heaved a big sigh of relief. For banks it meant more business.

Emboldened by its success, Citicorp rolled this service out in other markets. This was perhaps the first banking solution that was tested in India and then rolled out in the global market. This reaffirmed CK's belief that India was the hotbed for innovations and his proposition to MNCs that 'if you can succeed in India, you can succeed everywhere'.

Citibank renamed this banking solution as *Bank-at-Work* and launched it in New York in 2001. Its then Chairman Sandy Weill was impressed and decided to take it to UK, Singapore, the Philippines, Russia, Thailand and Poland. *Bank-at-Work* has close to three million customers globally.

Suvidha was a trail blazer. In 2002, Standard Chartered launched a supply chain finance scheme for the electronics, chemicals and auto industries in India. Its instant success led to the launch of similar products in other markets. Deutsche Bank pioneered the concept of in-sourcing corporate cheque issuance in early 2000. Under this facility, Deutsche Bank took complete responsibility of printing and issuing cheques for dividend payments and other services to shareholders for its corporate clients. After its success in India, the bank rolled it out in other Asian markets in 2001. It also took its Registrar and Transfer Agent (RTA), which offers a one-stop shop (custody, fund accounting, registrar and cash management) for asset management companies, in 2006, to its clients in Taiwan, the Philippines, Dubai and Vietnam after trial in India.

Citibank also established e-Serve International Ltd. formerly known as Citicorp Securities & Investments Ltd. in India, for its BPO activities. e-Serve provides IT-enabled solutions to the financial services industry, supported by the latest technology and its robust infrastructure for volume-intensive processing and the customer care needs in over 25 countries.

One of the earliest adopters of the BoP business concept was General Electric. GE's growth was shaky in the late 90s and its medical equipment division needed a fresh wave of products. Sensing that the momentum was shifting away from the West, GE set up its biggest lab outside the US in Bangalore called the John F. Welch Technology Centre in 2000. Among its early products for the emerging world was a low cost ECG machine. For a long time, GE's ECG machine was a monstrous 65 pounds heavy and $10,000 a piece. The ECG machine was literally shrunk to cater to rural India – three pounds in weight with printer attached, portable and connected to wireless and costing only $800. It has now been approved for sale in Europe and the USA.

Networking giant Cisco launched a low-cost platform for pushing education and healthcare services on broadband. With its second big R&D hub in Bangalore, India has become a sounding board for products aimed at emerging markets. *"We see India as a litmus test for our emerging market strategy. If we can be successful here, we can be successful anywhere,"* Jeff White, Cisco India head of operations told the media, echoing CK's vision of the new normal.

"My mandate is to drive innovation in India for the rest of the world. We want to develop products here so that we can take them to other emerging markets," he said. Cisco developed a set-top box and a new broadband platform aimed at innovative technology at lower price points. John Chambers, Cisco Chairman, told media that *"We are not here for labour arbitrage. This is where the future direction of the company is going to come from."*

GE, Cisco and a few other R&D companies, especially in pharma and biotech, are crowding out Indian companies from access to top scientific talent with better work conditions and incentives. But then, in a globalized world with a global consumer, does it matter who comes out with a useful and affordable product?

Fortune AT the BoP to Fortune WITH the BoP

Clearly, the BoP concept is CK's biggest contribution to the world. But, it is simply NOT about demand and supply to a certain section of consumers. Its underlying motive was to lift people out of poverty into the mainstream of the global economy.

CK could not hide his smile when an interviewer at *Knowledge@Wharton* online magazine asked whether he could see visible impact of his BoP idea in October 2009. *(http://knowledge.wharton.upenn.edu/article.cfm?articleid=2356)*. Wharton Publishing had just then released an updated version of the 2004 *'Fortune at the Bottom of the Pyramid'* with more case studies which firmly proved CK's theories right.

CK said: *"The impact has been interesting and profound in many ways – much more than one could have expected."* Adding, *"I asked 10 CEOs of companies as diverse as Microsoft, ING, DSM, GSK and Thomson Reuters to essentially reflect on whether the book has had some impact on the way they think about the opportunities. Uniformly, everybody said not only that it has had some impact, but that it changed the way they approach innovation and ... new markets."*

The BoP idea has travelled to the high tables of global institutions such as The World Bank, UNDF [United Nations Development Fund], IFC [International Finance Corporation] and USAid. **For the first time, they accepted the idea that involvement of the private sector was critical for development.**

Interestingly, when it was conceptualized, it was meant for MNCs wanting to expand their business in the emerging markets. To their pleasant surprise, CEOs discovered that the poor and the lower middle class in developed countries too were a sizable market for low-cost-high-quality products. For example, Netbooks, a $200 computer, sold more than two million pieces in the US alone in 2008.

So what major lessons did companies learn through serving poor consumers? When *'Fortune at the BoP'* was published in 2004, there was a fair amount of scepticism yet CEOs could not walk away from the compelling videos and the stories in the book. CK's compelling rebuttals of criticisms did put many of them to rest. He cleared the myths and the path for profound rethinking about the opportunities at the BoP.

The way the wireless cellular phone industry worked in India gave the idea a big booster shot. For the first time in human history, four billion of the six billion people were connected. The dramatic shift took place across the world too -- all the companies across markets -- Celtel, Safaricom, MTN, Airtel, Reliance, Globe are making money. So the first lesson was if you can find the right sweet spot in terms of business models, there is a really a huge and very profitable opportunity.

BoP markets also started to become extraordinary sources of innovation. For example, Safaricom offered mobile cash allowing poor Kenyans, who did not have access to banks, to transfer money from A to B by text messaging. By 2009, seven million consumers were involved in this. Filipino maids working in Singapore were sending money home through an SMS message. From simple money transfers, this technology is being extended for application in public health, education and even entertainment like video downloads for a few cents. Governments are using this platform to transfer subsidies directly to the poor who do not have bank accounts. This is also helping cut down leakages significantly which have dogged the subsidy mechanism in poor countries.

In fact, what we are seeing is only the beginning of a radical transformation of how consumer – provider engagement will unfold in the coming years. **CK's favourite line that the poor too today have the same access to advanced technology as the rich, for the first time in history,** will manifest in many more ways. *"I see infinite possibilities, and I believe a lot of these innovations are going to come from BoP markets because there is a necessity there,"* he said.

CK's BoP business model innovation had run its full course in about a decade and needed refurbishing. Fortunately for CK, Stuart Hart and Ted London, his colleagues at the University of Michigan, were ready with a draft of *'Next Generation Business Strategies for the Base of the Pyramid: New Approaches for Building Mutual Value'*. They had asked CK to write a chapter, but his poor health didn't let him do that. The book was released in 2011, a year after CK passed away.

The authors, who dedicated the book to CK, say that the first-generation 'Bottom of the Pyramid' (BoP) ventures focussed primarily on finding a fortune at the BoP by selling existing goods to and sourcing familiar products from the world's four billion poorest people. But many of these initiatives did not scale, and some even 'failed outright'. *"But through that experience, crucial lessons have been learnt."*

This book is almost like a manual for new generation BoP entre-preneurs. It shows how to apply and build successful business ventures using 'second-generation BoP innovations, techniques, and business models.' They focus extensively on creating *"sustainable business ecosys-tems, design new technologies with the BoP in mind, and even transform entire sectors through collaborative entrepreneurship."*

True to CK's credo – this is Next BoP practices. The seemingly sub-tle but significant shift which Stu and Ted have introduced is – from Fortune AT the BoP to Fortune WITH the BoP.

Deepa Prahalad believes the lasting impact of the BoP theory is that few companies in any part of the world today deny the ability of the world's poor to make intelligent choices. Today, companies are debat-ing about **how** to design for the BoP (and competing fiercely to do so), not wondering whether the poor 'need' new technology or will pay for quality products. This transition is perhaps the ultimate validation of the BoP theory.

Bill Gates, former Microsoft Chairman, sums it up aptly: *"Prahalad challenges readers to re-evaluate their pre-conceived notions about the com-mercial opportunities in serving the relatively poor nations of the world. The Bottom of the Pyramid highlights the way to commercial success and societal improvement."*

It's certainly too early, Deepa says, to tell whether these efforts, com-bined with policy efforts, will actually reduce poverty over time. How-ever, empowering the poor and inspiring the entrepreneurs and people inside companies to do more was no small feat. In evangelizing the idea of the BoP, CK may also have helped to embed some of his unique traits in the organizations he worked with – compassion, humility and a deep desire to help others.

Sustainability - Innovation's New Frontier

MR Rangaswami and Ram Nidumolu had written an 85-page report in 2008 after interviewing 30 Corporate Eco Forum (CEF) member companies about how they were addressing environment and ecology issues. MR had set up the Corporate Eco Forum in 2007 to bring businesses, NGOs, academia and the government under one platform to influence policy at both the organization and government levels. CK was a mentor to the project and once the report was out, he asked MR for a copy and read it on one of his long-haul flights. On the way back, CK drew an outline for an article and showed it to MR and nudged him to send it to the Harvard Business Review.

MR remembers the day when CK handed him the rough outline for the article. *"I said, wow, how's that I hadn't seen it. He was able to pull this out of this material and that was the brilliant thing about CK, **the ability to take complex ideas and bring out a framework, draw out its essence and make it understandable to C-level executives."** They were pleasantly surprised to see their article as the cover story in HBR September 2009 with the title 'Why sustainability is now the key driver of innovation'.

When MR invited CK to mentor him at the CEF in 2007, CK's reply was not 'yes' or 'no'. It was, *"What should we do?"* With CK on board, CEF looked turbo-charged. *"CK looked at all the mundane literature and discussion points meant for the first annual meeting and made them very provocative,"* MR remembers.

Traditionally, CK followed a successful paper with a book. After HBR published their article as the cover story in 2009, CK called MR and seeded the thought of a book. But his illness meant the idea had to wait, but with his unexpected demise, the authors will miss CK whenever they plan to put one together.

Nearly four years after the publication of the article, Ram Nidumolu and MR were elated to hear that it was selected for the prestigious Citations of Excellence Awards for 2013 as one of the top 50 cited articles by Emerald Management Reviews. The article had already become one of the most popular re-prints in HBR.

The most cited articles were picked from a vast database of more than 300,000 article abstracts from the top 300 management publications worldwide between 2009 and 2013. Their article had emerged as the most original and ground-breaking piece of work in the area of sustainability, a field that is coming into its own only now.

In the article, the authors argued that *"Sustainability is a mother lode of organizational and technological innovations that yield both bottom-line and top-line returns. Becoming environment-friendly lowers costs because companies end up reducing the inputs they use. In addition, the process generates additional revenues from better products or enables companies to create new businesses. In fact, because those are the goals of corporate innovation, we find that smart companies now treat sustainability as innovation's new frontier."*

These findings led to a decline in scepticism, especially among CEOs who typically fear short-term consequences of adopting sustainability practices on their balance sheet. The authors argued that their quest has already begun to transform the competitive landscape, as companies are focusing on redesigning products, technologies, processes, and business models. Yet, it seems like early days for these ideas to sink into the organizational DNA.

After CK died in April 2010, the Corporate Eco Forum instituted an annual '*The C.K. Prahalad Global Sustainability Leadership Award*' the same year. Interestingly, most of the award winners, from 2010 to 2013, stated that they were influenced by CK's strong belief in 'Doing Well by Doing Good' ever since 'The Fortune at the Bottom of the Pyramid' idea became mainstream thinking and that sustainability was an extension of that principle.

The wide spectrum of award winners since 2010 indicates that indeed serious commitment and efforts are being made across the world on sustainability. CEF hopes that their stories will inspire many more to eventually become a movement at least in a decade. **Marrying sustainability with business innovation has become an imperative.**

When the corporate world was still trying to understand corporate social responsibility, CK asked them to leap-frog into thinking and acting on Sustainability. The speed with which the US picked it up is because CK, and a few others, smartly showed that there was profit in it. **By linking innovation with sustainability, he was able to take it to the board room quicker than anyone thought it would.** It looks as if science and business are gearing themselves up to face the sustainability challenge. However, they need the backing of public policy big time.

Chapter 6

Indian IT --
The Value Driver

I believe India is going to re-write the meaning of manufacturing quality with intelligent components. **CK Prahalad**

We have more than 50 percent global market share of all outsourcing, 70 percent IT-enabled service and one-third market share of business process outsourcing (BPO). We have a target $300 billion dollars for 2020. **Som Mittal, Nasscom President**

My firm belief is that the software product industry will lift India out of its poverty. **Sharad Sharma, former CEO of Yahoo! India R&D**

Looking back, he was asking midgets to behave like giants. Today, many of the very same midgets have transformed themselves into giants. **Subroto Bagchi, Chairman, Mindtree Ltd.**

"If you were a painter, how should you price your painting?" CK thundered in his trademark booming voice to a room full of software industry leaders in Mumbai in 1997. The way the software industry priced its output in the mid and late 1990s was akin to a painter charging for the oil and the canvas, and then some more for the labour, all at actual cost. *"Going by that logic, how much do you think should the price of an MF Hussain painting should be?"* CK asked in a taunting tone.

CK compelled Indians to respect their own work if they expected the world to respect them by stating *"What you are doing today is cost plus pricing; what you need to shift to is value minus pricing."* Senior IT leaders think this strategic shift in their mindset early on helped the sector's meteoric growth from a few hundred million dollars in revenue in the early 1990s to close to $100 billion in 2012. If they had not done this, India may have ended up like China has in manufacturing – a low cost, high volume software producing country.

This chapter celebrates Prof. CK Prahalad's relatively less known but pivotal role as a catalyst of the Indian IT sector; how astutely he shaped the direction and mindsets right from the days when the seeds were sown in the mid 1980's, in the words of IT leaders themselves. It also tries to observe its current challenges and wonders if business leaders can depend on CK's formula as they explore new possibilities. It tries to offer a ringside view of the interesting facets and anecdotes that have embellished the Indian IT sector's journey. Last and perhaps most importantly, the objective of this chapter is to celebrate the successes of leaders who dreamt and toiled to create and nurture India's knowledge sector with CK as their guiding star.

It's interesting how CK turned into a crusader for the IT sector. It was as if he knew what was in the offing. He took upon himself the onus of playing multiple roles with the single-minded focus of supporting a mega business opportunity out of India's disparate resources. As a *provocateur*, he pushed Indians to think big. As an accomplished global thought leader of strategy, and author of management bestsellers, he acted like a bridge where global demands and opportunities met Indian entrepreneurial dreams. As a guide, he stayed with the sector all through its formative years to ensure that it didn't stray into dangerous alleys. As a coach, he mentored senior business leaders to think big all the time and wade through uncertainties. As a student, CK learnt from Indian entrepreneurs' experience in real time and had empathy for managers. As an astute networker, he connected Indian leaders' aspirations to global corporations' needs. And, as a true friend, he enjoyed the camaraderie of several leaders and, yet, didn't hesitate to reprimand them for their faults.

It's rare for a management thinker to have had such an uncanny grasp of the impact technology would have on business and society much before information technology started to radically change the way business was run. What's more, CK had a strong belief about India's ability to play a key role in the way global IT evolved and tried hard to pass on this belief to business leaders. It appears that he succeeded in doing it.

It's apparent that CK's mission of building a new India through business transformation was sector neutral. It was a happy coincidence that a good number of the business leaders who attended all his CEO forums were from the IT sector.

Master Class

Narayana Murthy, Infosys co-founder and Indian IT's icon, and CK were good friends from their IIM Ahmedabad days. Mr. Murthy keenly followed CK's rise in the global management thought leadership space and was well aware of the profound impact his books had on business leaders in the 1990s. In 1996, the year *Competing for the Future* hit the stands, Mr. Murthy invited CK to take a master class for some 60 IT business leaders and CEOs in Mumbai.

Co-authored with Gary Hamel, *Competing for the Future* had rattled global business leaders out of their comfort zones, but offered a ray of hope to Indian business leaders. It explained how new competitive realities had ruptured industry boundaries, had overthrown standard management practices and were rendering conventional models of strategy and growth obsolete. The authors urged companies to create their own future and envision new markets instead of trying hard to get a share of the existing markets. **The words 'create your own markets' rang loudly in CEOs' ears.**

This master class is of historic significance to the Indian IT sector and through it to the Indian economy. It laid the foundation on which Indian IT built its dreams. It was also the first attempt to appeal to the collective wisdom of Indian IT business leaders to project themselves in the global market as one force. CK's strong message was *'sell the India story first to global markets and all other marketing pitches could come later'*. He goaded them to focus on the value Indian companies could offer and focus less on the cost advantage factor.

Nasscom President Som Mittal, who was heading Digital Equipment then, remembers: *"CK provided enormous perspective that we shouldn't just be happy with what we have already started doing. We should aim high. It was no surprise that in 1998, Nasscom and McKinsey published our first report with an audacious revenue forecast of $50 billion by 2008, when we were doing just $3-4 billion. This vision changed our own ambitions and aspirations and we started articulating it in our forums. Until we achieved the $50 billion (we were only two quarters late) in 2008, everyone thought this target was only in theory."*

Ashok Soota, head of Wipro Technologies from 1991 until late 1999, remembers CK appealing to the eager IT entrepreneurs not to try to be all things to all people, which he thought would certainly result in them serving only the low-end segments. ***"You got to see where the value lies. You got to position yourself rightly and that can come to you only if you have deep domain knowledge."*** Mr. Soota says: *"I can tell you that, years before anybody talked to me about domain knowledge in software, it was CK. Everyone was only focussing on how fast the business was growing at 70-80% a year. Strangely, our customers too were rushing to teach us how to grow but didn't ask us - what's your knowledge?"*

'Never think of resources as your strength or lack of it as weakness. If you are doing it intelligently, it's not a problem'. This mantra of CK went over the heads of most CEOs at CEO Forums but once they started executing it they realized its power. They started to feel a deep sense of self-belief that Indian companies could indeed compete in the global market place. Mr. Soota says his learning from CK stayed much longer as he moved on to launch his own business ventures. *"You could see how those*

thoughts developed and built confidence among a lot of us and surely had a ripple effect of impacting so many people." CK made us think solutions and 'verticalisation' leading to Industry based go-to-market structure/approach instead of horizontal/technology approach.

CK had a distinct style of getting his point cut right through to the bones of the sceptics. Mindtree Limited co-founder Subroto Bagchi recollects CK's opening remarks at an IT conference: *"He was giving them (CEOs) a good bashing for not understanding the essence of what he called value minus pricing."*

It's apparent that CK didn't simply lecture in forums. He went around the country like a missionary to industry associations of all kinds, colleges and conferences, gave umpteen media interviews to enlighten Indians about the immense possibilities ahead of them. ***"Looking back, he was asking midgets to behave like giants. Today, many of the very same midgets have transformed themselves into giants,"*** Bagchi wrote in his tribute to CK in his blog.

Companies which took the easy path of quick deals through price cuts irritated CK no end. He would say that unless they stepped out of their comfort zone they wouldn't make it. **He also emphasized how a pricing game could kill everyone and that they needed a high profit strategy so that they could invest in the future**. He came across as their worst critic, but the very next minute he ensured that his positive affirmations galvanized his clients and friends to exceed their potential several times.

CK's formula for Indian IT

- You cannot take global IT giants head on in what they do. Choose areas where they are weak. First look for the weakest brick in the wall to make an entry. This way, you could pull down the wall brick by brick.
- Set very high ethical standards. You have to prove in India that you can do well by doing good.
- Focus on value, not price.
- Focus on enriching domain knowledge, not percentage of growth.
- Lack of resources is not a weakness, lack of aspiration is.

- Marketing innovation is as important, if not more, as technology or business model innovation.
- Join forces to compete as a nation, do not undercut one another.

Many IT CEOs insist that the grounding they received very early on in their journey in how to build a vibrant business and sustain it has kept them in good shape so far and would continue to be relevant as they face newer challenges post 2014. It's interesting how CK's 'value' lesson keeps coming back to haunt Indian IT as it increasingly faces the threat of commoditization. For example, Infosys renamed its global delivery model on which it built its business for two decades as the Value Global Delivery Model (VGDM) in late 2013.

Infosys Campus

It appears CK and Narayana Murthy belonged to a mutual admiration club. CK's daughter Deepa Prahalad remembers Mr. Murthy and his wife Sudha Murthy calling on CK in his hotel suite a day before the inauguration of the Infosys campus in Electronics City in Bangalore in 1993. Mr. Murthy was all praise for CK for his achievements as a globally-renowned management thinker. CK returned the compliment by telling Mr. Murthy that his achievement was far greater because he had done it in India and set an example for many others.

Subroto Bagchi considers the inaugural function of the Infosys Campus as a landmark in Indian IT's journey. There were several firsts and the most important was Mr. Murthy inviting all IT leaders, including competitors to a dialogue where CK was the chief guest. It was perhaps the beginning of a strategic co-habitation between the top IT companies – Infosys, Wipro, TCS, HCL and a few others. CK was confident that the IT industry would take India forward because, *"You have a chance to be world class from the beginning. This is one industry we have to be world class even to participate."*

At this event Mr. Murthy pledged publicly for the first time to build 100 millionaires. He sure kept his word. There were more millionaires among Infosys shareholders in 2014 than any other company in India.

This was also the beginning of the stock option boom that made the IT sector glamorous for hundreds of thousands of youth.

Infosys' ethical business model impressed CK and he wanted everyone else to adopt it. *"You have to prove in India that you can do well by doing good."* The perception in India had been that if you did well, you had some connections. Infosys set the precedent to prove this wrong. Mr. Murthy often said that for companies to be financially successful and good, leaders had to demonstrate that values matter at every turn and with every employee. *"A clear conscience is the softest pillow on which you can lay your head down at night,"* is Mr. Murthy's favourite line to his employees.

The Tata Consultancy Services (TCS) didn't have to struggle with the ethics and transparency issues because it was a Tata group company – known for their legendary best practices.

Unlike the other big IT companies Wipro was a brick and mortar company and was into computer hardware before it decided to enter the software development and IT solutions business. Says Mr. Bagchi: *"Wipro's challenges to practice ethics in business were higher. It had to live with the crocodile every day. Yet, the fact that the company stood for values and best practices was commendable."*

It's apparent that CK was drawn to the IT sector much before the others because of its strong focus on values. It was easier for him to connect global corporations with Indian IT companies and by early 2000, several blue chip global companies were lining up to have a direct presence in India. Today, the Indian IT sector is much more diversified with MNC companies like IBM and Accenture employing more people than most Indian companies. They have become an integral part of the Indian IT story. The Indian IT canvas now is much larger, deeper and diverse and doesn't revolve around a handful of listed companies.

You Don't Know How Good You Are

In the initial years, IT leaders would get really foxed when CK told them repeatedly that they were very good at what they did but they didn't know that and he had to prove it to them. For example, Indian companies were training thousands of engineers, who were picked up from diverse background and cultures across India every year, as if they knew how to do that for years. CK showed them that what they were doing was not even attempted anywhere else in the world. They were training close to 100,000 software engineers a year in their giant facilities. The Infosys' Global Education Centre in Mysore, for example, is the largest in the world with training facilities for 14,000 people a year.

Indian IT took a few years to earn the respect of the world for the quality and depth of its services. Despite that, even until 2005, India was referred to in the US as 'nothing more than a country of 'body shoppers or cyber coolies'.' CK asked the IT community not to take this as an insult but to be proud of the 'ridicule' because it was not as easy as it was made out to be.

Even when popular media and disgruntled executives launched their invectives on cheap Indian labour, Mr. Bagchi says that in his thirty years of his experience in IT, at no point was he made to feel small by global CEOs. In fact, the respect the Indian IT sector got was seldom enjoyed by other industries and there was clearly a rub off.

On the body shopping jibe, Saurabh Srivastava, Chairman of Steria, India, co-founder of Nasscom, remembered CK's words during his talk at the Prof. CK Prahalad Memorial Lecture - TiE Delhi 2012 – *"I am not quite sure you know what you have actually done. You have seriously innovated when everybody said we hadn't innovated. What you have done is, you have taken the entire chain of software from the customer to the last line of code, you have disaggregated the chain and you have then taken different pieces and done them differently and put it together again. This is the reason why even though you have grown from $50 million to $ 100 billion (in 20 years) you are still growing at 20-30% a year."*

When everybody looked at India's software service delivery as a dumb back office job, CK looked at it as innovation. Addressing University of California (UCLA) students in 2005 he said: *"For those of you who have been involved in software for a long time we have assumed that we have to co-locate software workers in order to produce high quality. What the Indian software industry has demonstrated is you can produce better quality by creating off-site, on-site capabilities by remote delivery."*

When CK got the ball rolling In the 1990s very few MNCs had a direct presence in India. It was not part of their original script. Mr. Bagchi recollects: *"When global technology companies saw Wipro, Infosys, TCS and others shed their inhibition and play on front foot to establish India as an IT destination, MNCs realized that they needed direct presence here. They saw how these technology companies could work in India without paying a bribe. Until then, no MNC would come to India. India was a black box."*

The tipping point was when General Electric decided to set up their only R&D centre outside the United States in Bangalore in September 2000. Called The John F. Welch Technology Centre (JFWTC), the team has more than 4000 engineers and scientists working on cutting edge technologies for the world. It heralded a rush of engineering services, chip design, social media companies. Jack Welch, CEO of GE then had famously said that *'locking into Indian brains was a matter of competitive advantage'.*

During CK's three-year stint with Microsoft India in mid-2000, Ravi Venkatesan, Chairman of Microsoft India between 2004 and 2012, says CK shaped Microsoft's strategy for the emerging markets. CK believed that to succeed in emerging markets and to succeed in India, you really have to have a much stronger middle of the pyramid and bottom of the pyramid play – you can't just sell software only to the large companies and hope to make it big.

CK's point of view was – **you need to defeat piracy through innovation of the business model, and stop wasting your time fighting it.** *"That was a powerful idea, and we spent time on how to change pricing, how to try experiments where piracy could be defeated through technology. Some of those were quite successful, some were not,"* says Mr. Venkatesan.

Microsoft changed the pricing not by bringing down prices but by making lower cost versions available. It's interesting how, despite significant advertising spend, the subsidized version of Windows didn't catch on. But it helped bring down software piracy in India to 63% from 75 %.

Interestingly, Ravi Venkatesan thinks **CK anticipated the shift of computing from a computing oriented paradigm to a communications oriented paradigm early on.** Around 2006-07, the communications piece was an adjunct to a computing device. CK anticipated that communications device could be the core which would also do computing. Today, smart phones are more powerful than desktop PCs five years ago.

Everyone's Guru

CK would surprise everyone with his keen eye for the unknown. Som Mittal says: *"This is quite unique because you have people who either understand the global part or the India part but rarely somebody who is straddling both — to be able to look at the intersection of India's strengths and capabilities and global requirements."*

Looking at the amount of time and energy CK invested with the leaders of Indian IT sector, it might seem he was doing this full time. CK was a consultant to Wipro for five years, mid to late 1990s; was a mentor to HCL founder Shiv Nadar, was close friends with TCS Vice Chairman S Ramadorai, Infosys founders Narayana Murthy and Nandan Nilekani; he was on the board of Microsoft India helping the company in its fight against piracy innovatively.

Lakshmi Narayanan, Vice Chairman, Cognizant Technology Solutions Corp. wrote in Wall Street Journal: *"His power of abstraction was phenomenal: You could present him a 20-page report and he could give you back a post-it with a simple phrase on it, so concise and powerful that you could stick it everywhere and get everyone to follow it for years to come. Cognizant and I, personally, have a great deal to thank him for."* Clearly, the IT companies CK advised, consulted and was friends with are pretty much the leaders of Indian IT today.

S Ramadorai and CK spent decades learning from each other. *"I often felt his ideas straddled two worlds, they were both globally relevant and yet very India specific. He was a firm believer that technology had to be embedded in every aspect of business."*

CK's last book *'The New Age of Innovation – Driving Co-created Value Through Global Networks'*, Mr. Ramadorai says, *"....struck a chord because I saw several parallels between its concepts and what TCS was attempting to do at that time (early years of 2000). The book spoke about how innovation will be driven by the seamless integration of strategy, business processes, and technology and people factors. At TCS we were talking at that time about both going beyond technology innovation into innovation of business models and the process and delivery."*

TCS is a pioneer of India's software sector and has managed to retain its leadership position consistently in India. It is close to achieving its aspiration to be the 10th largest global IT company with a market cap of $100 billion. Marketing guru Jagdish Sheth credits TCS' incredible run to two major factors – offering five-star hotel style customer service and entering markets like China very early, even before anyone thought it was a business opportunity for software.

Indian IT 2.0

The information technology journey is perhaps the most gratifying story in Indian business history. The legendary zest of Indian entrepreneurs, frugal innovation, a near mastery in managing ambiguity and chaos, along with a friendly global business cycle between 2000 and 2008, contributed to Indian IT becoming a force to reckon with.

Mr. Mittal says: *"In a lot of ways, we created the IT industry. It wasn't there; it wasn't given to us on a platter. We created this sector by skill, by building confidence, trust, quality processes, security practices and much more. Here's an industry, which, in lot of ways, CK coached in the early years, gave us a vision on how we could compete for the future at a global scale."*

Som Mittal's face lights up when asked about Indian IT's numbers even if he has to repeat it any number of times. *"I'm happy to say that exports in 2013 would be $ 85 billion dollars, an increase from USD 75 billion in 2012, which is significant considering the global economic conditions. We have more than 50 percent global market share of all outsourcing, 70 percent IT-enabled service and one-third market share of business process outsourcing (BPO). We have a target of $300 billion dollars for 2020."*

So far, Indian IT and ITES companies have been focussing on the Fortune 1000 organizations and have been going after big deals. In the next phase, the much larger middle segment appears juicy - hence Som Mittal's aggressive $300 billion revenue target for 2020.

Indian IT still has enough fire in it to last a few more years. The big question is - has rapid growth and financial success made it difficult for Indian IT leaders to stay agile and reinvent quickly? Many IT companies, including some of the big five, are struggling to recover from the bruises inflicted by the 2008 global recession. The threat of commoditization is real and the nimbleness needed to explore newer frontiers is wanting. The painfully slow recovery of the western markets has added to their woes.

The next phase of Indian IT has already started taking shape. This time it will be led by hundreds of medium sized enterprises unlike the big five so far. The focus is shifting from back-office operations to a much wider canvas involving cloud, analytics, big data, mobility, infrastructure and knowledge processes.

A visible trend would be the declining revenue contribution from project-based and staff augmentation deals to significant strides in developing industry-specific BPO services through acquisitions and/ or organic growth. Integrated services play – applications, infrastructure and BPO could offer a better handle on clients' IT-business process. **The good news is that the Indian technology sector in 2014 is the most globalized and will swim or sail along with its global partners.**

Clearly, Indian IT leadership too is in a transition. As the baton changes hands from the founders to either their children or professional managers, it will be interesting to watch how the second generation IT leaders carry forward the great job of their fathers and founders.

Just like in most other spheres, a New India is emerging in the technology space. India is witnessing a start-up revolution in product development, mobile app development and delivery services. The new generation of young entrepreneurs with sparkle in their eyes, are still battling the business unfriendly eco-system. Venture funding is meagre, the industry needs greater access to working capital and could do with fewer laws and regulations.

The journey to Indian IT 2.0 has been robust but for it to reach Nasscom's target of $300 billion by end of this decade, a significant re-imagining is needed.

Affordable Computing

Historian Ramachandra Guha says it was strangely, Karl Marx who first stated that technology would have the most profound impact on societies. The Government of India's role in creating public assets has had minimal impact largely due to massive leakages and mal-governance. Can technology make amends and help reclaim lost ground in fighting poverty, illiteracy and malnutrition? Technology is fast becoming a prominent inclusive player as well as a democratizing force. It could make bad governance difficult.

To CK, the bottom of the pyramid strategy with right technology (he hated the concept of appropriate technology) could move more poor out of poverty than the most brilliant piece of policy or legislation. The fact that the two are on the verge of a tipping point is probably the best news India has heard in recent years. Sharad Sharma, most recently CEO of Yahoo! India R&D says: *"My firm belief is that the software product industry will lift India out of its poverty."*

TCS' Mr. Ramadorai thinks CK's views on the possible impact of IT on democratizing education and skilling of youth are significant. *"He felt that given the challenges of India in terms of reach and scale, technology could be a big driver in addressing the lack of good quality content and lack of good faculty being accessible to people who needed it the most."* The hot topic just before CK passed away had to do with leveraging national rural broadband as a last mile solution and UIDAI for authentication as part of the model.

The Government of India's UIDAI (Unique Identification Authority of India) is in the process of creating a biometric identification database of all Indians (the *Aadhar* card), a more advanced identity system than currently available in many developed countries. This could be the force multiplier that India has been waiting for to achieve multiple objectives such as delivering subsidies and incentives directly to people so that the poor can become bankable and also give them the social status that comes with identity. The government innovated here by roping in Nandan Nilekani, co-founder of Infosys, to head this project with the belief that it needed the drive and efficiency of the private sector mind to accomplish public goals in good time. It has worked well and could perhaps be a model for other initiatives.

India is now looking at exploiting the happy convergence of IT software-hardware and telecom to address its pathetic primary education and healthcare system. Its bold tablet program of providing affordable tablets to school children with broadband connectivity may soon revolutionize education. The tablets could also take telemedicine and micro banking idea to the next level. This might need UIDAI-type management approach to achieve desired results.

By 2004-05 the big bottom of the pyramid (BoP) idea had got under everyone's skin. For small businesses applying IT to become efficient was very expensive. The word ERP (Enterprise Resource Planning) was so threatening that SME businessmen would dread even mentioning it. That's when CK's BoP influenced two Indian companies to take it on themselves to challenge big ERP MNCs' stranglehold.

Srikant Rao happened to bump into CK at Prof. Sadagopan's office at Indian Institute of Information Technology (IIIT), Bangalore in 2004. Srikant Rao says: *"Everyone at IIIT was talking about affordable IT. When we went to IIT Chennai it was affordable telecom. The question was – how can millions of Indian SMEs procure the same product, services that a big company could at a fraction of that price point? We took CK's concept of factorization, and we said let's factorize the cost. The challenge was how do we give the quality and the service of an IBM or an SAP? The only alternative was to unburden them by offering monthly fee structure, which a lot of them could afford. A viable business model appeared in front of us."* **CK told them to think about how to 'sachetize' it and once you build the model you have to scale without dropping the service quality.**

The Bangalore-based firm, Affordable Business Solutions (www.abs.in) has so far built 12 platforms for different verticals. It has been conservative in scaling up its customer numbers, which Srikant Rao says, will happen once the platforms take off seamlessly. Since after sales service is the critical factor here, ability to scale is becoming a major issue. ABS may have to disrupt this as well if it has to make a mark.

Chennai-based Ramco Systems has had the privilege of being mentored by CK for many years. It is today a leader in catering to Indian and global small businesses with a pay-as-you-use ERP solutions. It is taking advantage of cloud computing to offer anywhere ERP solution on a tablet.

Bangalore-based Tally Solutions has been a pioneer in providing affordable accounting software to small businesses. It has introduced an all-in-one affordable ERP along with its accounting software, *Tally 9.0.* It is arguably the most affordable one-stop IT solution for most businesses, especially micro and small businesses.

Seeing the viability of the affordable computing model, even the big players in the industry have introduced scaled down ERP or totally new affordable versions. TCS launched iON, which has the potential of breaking scale constraints faced by the other players with big investments in technology and marketing.

At last, Indian and even global small businesses can now have access to state-of-the-art IT business solutions using cloud and big data, without a big hole in their pocket.

IT – Auto, a Killer Combo

"IT shouldn't remain as IT but rather it should transform everything else," **was CK's favourite line.** One of his favourite charts at IT and manufacturing conferences showed two major sectors – automobile manufacturing and information technology outsourcing functioning separately in a big way in Bangalore, Chennai, Pune, and the Delhi region and growing at a fast pace. *"Why is it that the IT guys and the car guys aren't sitting together and trying to drive a revolution in telematics? What if you combine automotive domain knowledge, manufacturing quality, small batch capability, low cost and embedded software,"* he asked. *"I believe India is going to re-write the meaning of manufacturing quality with intelligent components."* These questions sparked the imagination of leaders of both the domains. What has emerged in the last eight years is an interesting journey of how the two are trying to make the best of their marriage.

Craig Barrett, Intel Chairman said that an automobile is nothing but chips on wheels; a plane is nothing but chips on wings. It meant that there would be a lot more of IT hardware and software inside automobiles. This requires the core competence of people in automobiles and software working together in one cluster. No other country has had this luxury like India. Japanese companies have been exceptionally good in automobile manufacturing but they depended on the US software companies for IT. Even in the US, auto companies and software companies are spread across different locations – auto in Detroit and software in California.

Prof. Sadagopan; Director of IIIT-Bangalore, one of India's key thought leaders and a teacher at premier Indian institutes of learning over the last three decades, has played a key role in Indian IT industry's evolution. Being an academic and a friend of CK and most of the IT leaders, he has had a ringside view of the industry's triumphs and failures. He says: *"One thing which was very striking with CK was his ability to connect the dots."*

He kept a close tab on how CK's provocation worked – how some have made it work and why and how some are still struggling. This makes for a very interesting, sometimes amusing, study of what businesses do when a powerful idea is presented to them.

The first few years were funny. Even before CK delivered his big idea, the Indian auto companies like the Tatas, Ashok Leyland, TVS and Mahindra had IT subsidiaries whose goal was to grab a pie of the rapidly growing IT software business. They were essentially competing with the big Indian IT players such as Infosys, Wipro, HCL and TCS and sulked at their inability to make a dent.

The Tatas started Tata Technologies, Ashok Leyland, a big player in the truck business based in Chennai, started Ashok Leyland Infotronics and TVS, another auto major in two-wheelers in Chennai, started TVS Electronics. CK said it should be the other way around. **Instead of automotive companies becoming poor cousins of Infosys or Wipro, they should start something which the big guys will not be able to do – merge competence of automotive expertise and IT expertise together and package it into a new form of core competence.** This was CK's masterstroke which was lapped up with glee.

The IT leaders turned out smarter. Infosys, Wipro and a few others, launched automobile practice and did well. Wipro is said to be more successful in terms of numbers because it has a much larger embedded systems group.

Ashok Leyland Informatics is doing well making interesting lighting and braking components. **The auto-IT combo's big day was when Bosch's Bangalore plant produced the Engine Management System (EMS) for Tata Nano.** Till then, EMS was used only in high-end cars. Mahindra & Mahindra's foray into the passenger car market also involved a strong focus on developing its own software.

The efficiency of Indian logistics is dependent on trucks. CK was troubled by the sight of long lines of trucks at entry check posts and the unacceptable period of time taken by them to ply between two cities. He believed that real-time mapping of truck movements could halve the time taken between Chennai and Kolkata if tax management could be streamlined using software. Today, better fleet management has improved supply chain efficiency. Online retail chains are offering same city delivery in 24 hours and inter-city delivery in two to three days.

What started as simple embedded software in cars or trucks, has now taken a leap with maps like Google Maps for spatial information system. When it is applied to slightly higher end logistics like courier, supply chain and technical engine management or the ability to improve fuel efficiency, we are entering a new world altogether.

Prof. Sadagopan was keen to try his hand in the IT – auto mix himself. When a project from the Department of Science and Technology, Government of India, came his way, he didn't want to let it go. The project was to build a system that could track the movement of city buses in Chennai using a satellite with the objective of improving its punctuality. *"We got an accuracy of about a minute within Chennai and an accuracy of five minutes for inter-city bus service plying between Chennai and Madurai,"* he says.

The group also perfected the LED technology which was used to inform commuters about bus schedules. The technology from this project is being used in most cities in India today. While Indore claims to have been the first to introduce the traffic management systems, Prof.

Sadagopan says it was not scalable. With cloud computing at play now, he suggests that a single company or a few companies should operate in several cities – individual cities operating their own systems, like it is done now, is inefficient. Prof. Sadagopan's team also fine-tuned the software such that, in case of an accident, it would automatically send a message to the nearest police station, hospital and insurance office. Pictures were also taken automatically.

In the age of 'Internet of Things', cars have very high intelligence. Google is experimenting with driverless cars, but for now, it is on the verge of doing useful things like preventing drivers from jumping the signal, jamming mobile phones if the driver wants to speak while driving, the engine refusing to start if the driver is drunk beyond a limit, and much more.

CK's masterstroke of an IT-Auto hub is definitely a work in progress with immense possibilities for India to join the cutting edge of global IT. It's a unique model that could be replicated anywhere.

Chapter 7

Distilling CK –
A Critique of his Published Work

By S. Manikutty
**(The author is an Adjunct Faculty, Indian Institute of Management,
Bangalore & Faculty, Indian Institute of Management,
Ahmedabad (Retd.).)**

Abstract

This article assesses the contribution of the late CK Prahalad to the field of strategy and management. It looks at his key works and shows their linkages and the way they built on the previous ones, to produce a consistent approach to management.

To assess and put in perspective the late CK Prahalad's contributions to strategic management is not easy. So vast was his canvas that it would be difficult to even rank his contributions in some order of importance. He coined many terms that have become common parlance, and in some cases popularised the use of terms that might have existed in some corner of the academic world, but were taken out, dusted and refurbished: 'strategic intent', 'loose bricks', 'next practices', 'co-creation' and of course, the two phrases for which most of the practitioners would remember him: 'core competence' and 'bottom of the pyramid'. Each of the ideas were not just developed and put in a journal; each was developed to a point at which it became a concept that could be put to practical use. That was how he was such a towering presence as much in the world of practitioners as in the world of academicians: he would be the centre of attention as much in a conference of Chief Executives as in an Annual Meeting of the Academy of Management, giving a key note address. And in every meeting, he had something new to say.

Early Work

CK Prahalad (or CK as he was affectionately known among his admirers) did his early work in International Business. In his 1985 article in *Harvard Business Review (HBR)* jointly authored with Gary Hamel, titled *'Do You Really Have a Global Strategy?'* Hamel and CK drew attention to the distinction between competing globally, doing business globally and being a global company. In this paper, his originality was evident: while earlier, International Business literature focussed on one business at a time, following the business strategy models of the Industrial Organization (I-O) school and the work of Michael Porter and his colleagues, Hamel and Prahalad pointed out how global firms not only derive advantage through global operations for particular products or groups of products, but compete *across* products and businesses, and *across* geographical areas, as for example, cross subsidising products or markets. Thus a French tyre manufacture could enter the US market but the US incumbent may not necessarily stop at defending its market share in US; it could retaliate by entering the tyre markets of Europe, hitherto a strong hold of the French manufacturer. The responses, moves and counter moves in the two cases are very different.

Also, firms may compete in one way in the function of manufacture, in another way in the function of distribution, and in a third way in marketing and advertising. Thus international competition needs to take into account these multiple dimensions, and having a global strategy would imply a holistic understanding of these dynamics.

In many ways, CK's work ran in parallel with another duo that made an indelible mark: Chris Bartlett and Sumantra Ghoshal. The idea of integration – responsiveness (IR) framework of Bartlett and Ghoshal took IB theory forward in a big jump, in gaining an understanding of how to resolve the conflicting needs of integrating operations across countries and gaining consistency on the one hand and the need for differentiating across different countries, on the other. CK's ideas of viewing multiple businesses and geographical regions concurrently were more complex to grasp, but provided a complementary perspective to those of Bartlett and Ghoshal. Sadly, to my knowledge, these two Indian giants – CK and Ghoshal never worked together.

Dominant Logic

The paper '*The dominant logic: A new linkage between diversity and performance*' by Bettis and Prahalad (1986) took a line which stands apart from his other work. They examined the reasons for inconsistent results on the results of diversifications by firms. Earlier researchers had seen diversification in terms of relatedness in terms of technology and/ or markets. Bettis and Prahalad introduced their notion of 'dominant logic' as an explanatory variable for determining the success of diversification. This was another concept that appeals intuitively but is difficult to measure. It referred to a schema of mental maps developed through past experience, and this forms the lens through which managers look at new businesses. It drew heavily from concepts in psychology such as operant conditioning, pattern recognition processes by the human brain, and cognitive biases. The dominant logic constraints the thinking of management, and the success of diversification would depend upon the willingness of management to revise their dominant logic consciously to what is needed for the new business. They introduced the notion of 'strategic variety' of the business portfolios of firms, this being roughly the business models or the key success factors in a business. The firm should have the ability to manage this variety.

This came at a time when managers were perplexed as to whether diversification indeed led to a performance improvement or not. Indeed, markets were even giving a thumbs down to diversification by marking down the stock prices of a firm after it announced a diversification decision, the so-called diversification discount. Yet many firms were doing well even after quoted unrelated diversification, while firms encountered serious problems even with related diversification. Ghoshal also had pointed out the role of the capability of management in managing their diversification, in their study of Indian and other companies as the most important determinant of the success of diversification, as for example, in his works *Individual Corporation* and *Managing Radical Change*. Bettis and Prahalad had advocated a specific area of this capability: ability to manage different dominant logics for different businesses at the same time.

The paper was not one that made a great impact in my view, certainly not what its rich content deserved. I suspect this was because the concept of dominant logic was difficult to grasp, and managers tend to attribute to themselves greater abilities to really understand the logic of new businesses or manage variety than they actually possess. Hence advocating better understanding of the dominant logics of new businesses or managing the variety perhaps did not attract much managerial attention. I suspect also that the relative lack of impact of this paper was due to its publication in *Strategic Management Journal*, not really a favourite read for practising managers.

Strategic Intent, Stretch and Leverage

The concept of strategic intent is widely popular, and it gained currency from his article with the same title in *Harvard Business Review* published in 1989. This concept went much further than specific strategic goals and milestones, but not so broad as organizational purpose; it was a sort of vision of what the organization's position in a business would be like at a future point. I found it hard to distinguish it from a broad strategic objective, and though executed in incremental steps, organizations do have a direction and consistency in their actions with a view to achieving the broad objective. Strategic intent implied also a stretch in the organization (a concept he developed later as 'stretch and leverage', see below) and its resources, with a view to achieving something not recognized as easily achievable. Strategic intent would thus be a stretched and clearly understood broad strategic objective of what a firm intended to achieve. It enabled a firm to strive to reach out to much greater heights than would be apparent from a traditional SWOT analysis.

Core Competence

What made Prahalad (and Hamel) famous was undoubtedly their 1990 landmark paper, 'Core Competence of the Corporation', published in HBR. This paper marked a fundamental departure from the 'outside to inside' thinking of traditional Business Policy thinkers, who started with environment, and went on to 'fit' the organizations' strengths and weaknesses to it. Resources were to be marshalled to achieve what was dictated to by the environment. The Resource Based View (RBV) scholars had already developed an 'inside out' thinking, viewing the resources of a firm as the starting point, but CK emphasised the need for combining these resources and stretching them to new areas and new lengths; combined with an ambitious strategic intent, a firm could do its tasks in a markedly distinct way from its competitors. The trick was to find what a firm can do in a distinct and superior way as compared to other firms *across* different activities or products. For example, CK cited Canon's ability to produce miniaturised versions of a wide variety of products. The test of a core competence was its applicability across a number of *different* products and businesses to produce distinct and competitively superior offerings.

The concept of core competence challenged the managers to view their firms as a portfolio of competencies rather than as a portfolio of businesses. The SBU concept, developed to enable decentralised functioning of a multi-divisional corporation, indeed had enabled setting of high levels of accountability and the development of general managers at a relatively early stage in their careers. But it also created individual islands, the SBUs, which stopped thinking beyond their own boundaries. The result was the inability of a corporation to leverage competences developed in one business into another. The SBU based companies in US grew more slowly as compared to Japanese companies which focused on application of certain competencies across businesses, gaining competencies in each. Core competencies, CKP argued, could be the means to get out of the tyranny of SBUs.

Core competence, like many of CK's concepts, made for easy understanding at an intuitive level but was a teacher's and researcher's nightmare. While the examples he cited were perfectly logical in retrospect, when practitioners tried to apply the concept in their own firms, and identity their core competences they found the going difficult. Actually, most of the practitioners thought they had found the core competencies of their companies, but most of the times these were so general as to be virtually useless: managers claimed their core competencies lay in project management, cost control or good financial management or even simple 'good management'. In practice, the actual identification of such competencies seemed difficult.

Strategy as Stretch and Leverage

The real utility of the concept of core competence was in my view, not to enable accurate identification of specific competencies in an organization as such, but to enable executives to think of possibilities rather than limitations. It challenged CEOs to explore new possibilities where they could leverage the competencies of their firms. That was the singular thing about CK: after an interaction with him, CEOs suddenly felt energised, and inadequate at the same time. He would not let smugness stay; he would continuously goad everyone to stretch and reach further and further.

He explicitly challenged them to do so in his 1993 HBR article (jointly authored with Hamel), *Strategy as Stretch and Leverage*. This paper argued that resources needed for achieving ambitious strategic goals would always be inadequate: the existing resources would have to be stretched. Several ways to do this were pointed out: concentrating resources and focussing them, accumulating new resources through extracting new ideas and borrowing from other companies; complementing resources through blending and borrowing; conserving resources through recycling, co-opting and shielding them from unnecessary risks, and recovering resources. Ambitious managements must know how to stretch resources without snapping the organization. This stretch happens mostly incrementally, and while it is under the overall direction set by the top management, its actual execution takes place at numerous levels in an organization. Thus, in a sense, the concepts of stretch and leverage helped to bridge the gap between those who saw strategy as essentially a purposeful top down exercise, and those who saw it as 'employment' from a series of not necessary connected incremental decisions.

The book *Competing for the Future* by Hamel and Prahalad put together the above ideas in a coherent way. The basic theme of the book was what he had been advocating in his earlier papers: we are reaching the end of incrementalism; further progress would only occur through completely innovative, out of the box thinking. Future cannot be predicted, but it can be *imagined* and made to happen. As the authors claim, this book, putting together in one place the numerous ideas developed by them over the years, was for activists and revolutionaries.

Hitting at the Bottom of the Pyramid(BoP)

A great ability of CK was to look at what everyone looks at all the time and yet see it differently. During his perambulations all over the world, he saw what a potential the BoP market held, and how some companies were exploiting it profitably. They were different companies doing different things, but he saw with astonishing clarity the commonalities in their themes. The idea of lower margin higher volume business was age old, but what he observed was that this was not the only way, there were many other ways of reaching out to the BoP. MNCs and even large local corporate saw BoP customers as 'unviable' and neglected them. He told them they could not only serve BoP, but also serve them *profitably*.

The key insight was that when serving the BoP, the firm does not start from the cost to determine the price; rather it has to start from what price the BoP consumers are willing to pay and work backwards to the cost at which the firm has to produce. Rarely will just a large volume production be sufficient by itself; it has to be combined with other innovations. In some cases (such as the Jaipur Foot), the design and materials have to be drastically modified to bring down the cost; the delivery (in this case, the fitment of the prosthetic limb) needs to be quick and effective; the needs and concerns of the poor need to be given due consideration. This might mean measuring the patient, producing the limb, fitting it and giving training to use it, all to be done in one day. Or in the case of Aravind Eye Hospital, to produce intra-ocular lenses (IOLs) at a cost of $5 when an imported lens (all IOLs were imported in the late 1970s) cost $80! The doctors' productivity could be enhanced from about 5 surgeries per day to 25 through a streamlined 'production' system; bringing patients from different villages, performing eye surgeries on them, and dropping them back in their villages; outreach activities and so on. Aravind performs half of its surgeries and treats about half of its outpatients *free* and without any grants or donations. Thus it could perform about 200,000 surgeries per year, at least half delivered to the truly poor.

In his celebrated book *The Fortune at the Bottom of the Pyramid* (Prahalad, 2005), CK argued that the BoP segment would indeed be unviable so long as companies do not change their business models; but if they are willing to relook at how they need to address this segment (sometimes through adaptation; sometimes through a completely new business model), then a fortune awaits them. The fortune arises from sheer numbers in this segment.

CK came out with a set of 12 guidelines for companies addressing the BoP segment. These are given in Box 1.

Box 1

Twelve Principles of Innovation for BoP Markets

1. Focus on price-performance combination instead of just price

2. Develop hybrid solutions. See how the latest technologies can be used.

3. Ensure scalability of BoP solutions, in building up[a scale and replicating across different environments

4. Conserve resources

5. Understand the functionality of the product in the new environment and adapt it

6. Process innovations such as logistics and special ways to segregate customers needing different kinds of value are also important

7. Reduce the skill demands at different stages

8. Create demand, educate customers

9. Make sure products work in drastically different environments

10. Understand the heterogeneity of the customer population

11. Ensure adequate distribution systems

12. Keep track of evolution in BoP markets and continuously modify your products/ processes.

The BoP concept had its share of critics, notably from CK's colleague at Michigan, Prof. Karnani (2009). They have argued that by enticing the poor to purchase 'non-essentials' – such as soap and shampoo, they are encouraging them to cut down on their consumption on essentials; it is more important to increase their purchasing power.

CK's response has been to emphasise the need for choice even at the BoP: let the poor choose to be clean or be dirty. No one can dispute that indeed increase in purchasing power is what is needed by the poor, but the poor often pay much more for products and services than the rich, as for example, for water. That is because these products are produced and distributed the same way for the poor as for the well to do. Indeed, by reducing costs to affordable levels through innovations, firms may actually increase their consumption basket and effective purchasing power.

It would seem that CK's book on BoP was primarily addressed to MNCs and large corporations only. Perhaps it is true that from a marketing point of view, in the book (published from USA), he did address this much larger reader population, but the book is as much applicable to local firms of quite different sizes. Indeed, out of 12 cases cited in his book, only four are multinationals, and even among them, HUL and ITC are quite independent companies in India, with a great deal of strategic independence given to the local firms. Even CEMEX's innovation was based essentially in its home country, Mexico.

Co-creation

The next big contribution by CK has been his idea of co-creation developed jointly with Venkat Ramaswamy and presented in their book *The Future of Competition* published in 2004. They argued for a changed line of thinking about the customers to be marketed to. The new idea was to move away from just catering to their needs to involving them in the different stages in the value chains of the product: starting from the design of the product, to its distribution and delivery and after sales service. They called it a movement from customer satisfaction to creating a new customer experience. This involved a different way of thinking by organizations: willingness to engage in a dialogue with the customer, providing them access to your information, and induce a much higher degree of transparency. Customers decide what kinds of products they want, and what kinds of risks they would like to take in the process. Modern technology makes it possible to produce an endless variety of products, all tailor made for individual customers: the so called 'Power of One' (a theme he developed in his last book, *The New Age of innovation*, coauthored with MS Krishnan in 2008). With his characteristic flair for innovative labeling of a new concept, he and Krishnan called this 'N=1', meaning individualized creation for each customer. They also pointed out that today the resources of companies are global, or 'R=G'. With these two mantras, they challenged companies to respond to the very different demands of customers, using the very different kinds of resources now made available with technology.

Actually, these ideas had already been introduced by managers. For example, already Dell had developed this model of letting the customers configure their own computers; Cisco had done a somewhat similar thing with routers. Many could be the applications where the design or delivery could be varied infinitely to suit individual customer tastes and even cars can be configured by the customers and manufactured for each separately, thanks to the modern automatized manufacturing process. Incidentally, it saves big money for the firm – the customers are doing part of the firm's work for free. Today many software products are beta tested and the views of customers elicited to solve the problems in the product – the inspection and rectification done free by the customers! Open source software and even reference books such as Wikipedia point to the scope of such involvement of customers at different stages of the value chain of products. The contribution of CK and his co-authors was to show how firms can involve customers creatively and at the right stages, so that customers can experience their contribution towards value creation. They summarized the three key trends in the coming years that would determine how customers would relate to institutions: collaboration, connectivity and the power of computing. Any firm that ignores these trends does so at its own peril.

The Future Belongs to Emerging Economies

The theme CK had latched on to in his last years was that the emerging economies such as India were the future leaders of the world. India, especially, held a special place in his heart and he never tired of reminding the audience what potential India had. He argued that the state of being less developed is actually an advantage, since emerging economies can leap frog over the less inefficient technologies and processes, and set up systems that were free of legacy baggage. They would be foolish to repeat the mistakes done by the firms of the developed world, but would have to develop their own innovative solutions.

Lately thinkers such as Jeff Immelt, Vijay Govindarajan and Chris Trimble have taken this theme into their concept of reverse innovation, where emerging economies in fact export new ideas and models to developed economies to be adopted by them. CK outlined a vision for India for the year 2022, or when India would be 75 years old after attaining Independence, and his 'My Vision for India @75' was indeed an inspiring, but practical presentation (See Box 2). He inspired audiences with stories of Aravind Eye Care System, Jaipur Foot, HUL's initiatives into the rural segment, with its Project Shakti, ITC's E-Choupal, ICICI's innovative health insurance policies for the diabetics, and so on, many felt he knew more about India, or even about their own cities than they did themselves. He urged Indians to take their rightful place in the world economy, for which constant innovation was the key. He kept reminding all about the sheer size of the Indian market, the ingenuity of Indian people, their capacity to take risks and their never-say-die attitude. He urged everyone to create a sandpit for themselves to play in, and develop new ideas. He pointed out how ideas from India (and other emerging economies) were influencing the developed world rather than the other way round. He continuously urged people to forget about the best practices and focus on the 'Next Practices' instead. He would never let anyone rest for a moment on one's laurels and feel complacent.

During his trips, he talked to many managers, workers and consumers, travelled widely to many interior locations, and saw not just what was there but also what everyone had missed. His ability to provide great ideas was unmatched, and he richly deserved being ranked as *'The Most Influential Business Thinker'* in 2009, by the leadership consulting firm, CrainerDearlove. Despite his punishing schedule, he found time

---

Box 2

My Vision for India @75: CKP

1. Build a skilled manpower: 500 million quality technicians; 200 million graduates

2. India becomes the home for 30 of the Fortune 500 firms

3. India accounts for 10 percent of global trade

4. India becomes a source of global innovations

5. It derives new models from the Bottom of the Pyramid

6. Ten Nobel prize winners by 2022

7. 500 world class cities

8. Becomes the new moral force for people around the world

Source: www.indiaat75.in

---

to come to Ahmedabad every year to deliver a lecture on his new ideas, organised by the Ahmedabad Management Association at the Louis Kahn Plaza of the Indian Institute of Management. It was amazing to see how every year he had so much new to say. At the time he passed away, he was working on a project, titled Empowered India @ 75 as a vision for the year 2022 for India. Each encounter with him was an energizing experience and, like Ghoshal, left behind him a trail of ideas.

Alas, such ideas will flow no more.

Chapter 8

Vision and Framework — India @ 75

(This speech was delivered by CK Prahalad in New York on August 15, 2007)

Yes, India@60 - we have accomplished a great deal and we have to celebrate. I know we will have a fun-filled week here in New York. I suggest that as we celebrate, we ask ourselves: What next? As we celebrate India@60, let us remember that all our accomplishments are in the past. *Leadership,* however, is about the future and it is about change. Leadership is about hope. So I decided not to dwell on the past 60 years but to focus on the future. I will focus on *India@75*, not India@60. My focus will be on what we can accomplish in the next 15 years, building on our successes during the first 60. More importantly, what will it take to accomplish these goals during that period?

I will share with you one person's optimism, one person's concerns and one person's approach to building a vibrant and just India@75. I would like start with what India@75 can be. Unless we are clear about the potential it is very difficult to undertake a difficult journey. I believe that India can and should actively shape the emerging world order. This demands that India must acquire enough *economic strength, technological vitality* and *moral leadership*. Just economic strength and technological maturity is not enough. We know that the Soviet Union and Nazi Germany had economic and technological muscle. They failed. Morality is an integral part of leadership. I am going to emphasize all three dimensions, in equal measure, in India's march to Her destiny.

The Potential of India@75:

1. India turns its population into a distinct advantage. India has the potential to build a base of 200 million college graduates – a portfolio of educated people in every discipline. This is just 16% of India's population. Further, I would like to see 500 million certified and skilled technicians. Implicit in this future is universal literacy. This is possible in fifteen years, if leaders focus on this goal as a priority[1]. Think about what this means. India will have *the largest pool of technically trained manpower anywhere in the world.* This must be the starting point for global leadership. If India fails in its educational mission, the rest of my vision for India cannot be realized.

2. India must become the home for at least 30 of the Fortune 100 firms. I know this is an audacious goal but it is possible.

3. India accounts for 10% of global trade. India can. We have to change our mindset. In fact Indians took a lot of pride when India was not affected by the 1997 Asian crisis. I said, at that time, that it is a sad commentary because if India was connected with the rest of the world, she would have felt the impact of the crisis. India must become connected with the rest of the world -- a critical step in influencing others and more importantly, the basis for learning from others.

4. India becomes a source of global innovations - new businesses, new technologies and new business models. The early evidence is already in. Increasingly India is becoming home for new business

models - very low capital intensity, extremely low fixed costs, and conversion of fixed costs into variable costs (as in the case of Airtel). The bottom of the pyramid, the 800 million Indians, can become a major source of breakthrough innovations[2].

5. India needs to focus on the flowering of arts, science, and literature. Why can't India have ten Nobel prize winners? I want to add that it would be all the better if it was for the work done in India - not just Indians getting the Nobel Prize for the work done elsewhere.

6. India becomes the world's benchmark on how to cope with diversity. It becomes a benchmark for the practice of universality and inclusiveness. India has the opportunity as she is home to all the major religions, 15 major languages and hundreds of dialects, and a complex range of cultures, food habits and rituals – all the diversity one can hope for. If India is not the laboratory to practice diversity and inclusiveness nobody else is. *India is the laboratory to the world.*

One could add to the list. The six big opportunities that I have identified, when accomplished would change the influence of India around the world. India has the potential. If this potential intrigues you, then we can move on to the next interesting question: How do we get there? What are the principles we have to start with?

Core Principle

I want to suggest three principles. The first one is relates to the essence of *entrepreneurial transformation.* I know that many would say that the potential of India@ 75 cannot be realized because we do not have the resources. I remember seven years ago I suggested a target of 10% growth. Many in India, including some very senior and extremely knowledgeable bureaucrats said that we don't have resources for 10% growth. The issue is not resources but the *balance between aspirations and the resources.* Every entrepreneur who is in this room knows that it is the conscious misfit between aspirations and resources that creates innovations and entrepreneurial energy. As a country, India must have *high and shared* aspirations. The last time she had a shared aspiration as a country was in 1929 when the leaders of the then Congress party declared their ambition as *Poorna Swaraj*. Since then, India has never had a national aspiration which every Indian could share. A shared aspiration is fundamental for changing India. There are only two ways to realize an aspiration that is greater than available resources. One is to *leverage resources* -- get more for every person and every rupee that you spend. Alternatively one could change the game, and change it to your advantage. That was Gandhi's genius. Not the traditional armed struggle against the British, but peaceful Satyagraha. The second principle which is equally important is to realize that we cannot get to the potential of India@75 by extrapolating what we did for the last 60 years, or even the last 10 years. *You cannot get there (India@75) from here (the current state)*. You have to imagine India@75, that I described first and then *fold that future in. Folding the future in rather than extrapolating the past is fundamental.* That is the reason I started by describing the potential of India@75. But that does not mean that we go from here to there in one step. We have to take small steps and clear steps, which are directionally right. Some steps may be experimental. We move with small steps but move with a sense of urgency and purpose. Third, do not only focus on best practices. If everybody benchmarks everybody else we will gravitate towards mediocrity. So I suggest a focus on *next practices*. That means we have to amplify weak signals, see a new pattern of opportunity and have the courage to pursue them.

The three principles are simple but powerful as a methodology for revitalizing India. We must start with:

a. Aspirations > Resources
b. Fold the Future in
c. Focus on Next practices.

These principles require us to think differently of both the *here and now* and certainly *about the future*. It forces us to develop a *distinct point of view*. A bold and energizing future for India cannot be created without a *shared point of view*. Incrementalism will not get us there. Let's not just attempt band-aid solutions. The key to becoming a leader in the world must begin by creating a shared commitment to aspirations supported by creativity, innovation and entrepreneurship.

The Developmental Context

What is the socio-political and economic context in which we have to accomplish this? I believe that during the next 10-15 years the debate in India will change rapidly. I have identified six areas where the direction of the debate and its resolution will be crucial for India to realize Her potential. The areas for consideration are:

1. Shift from abject poverty to income inequality
2. Shift from income levels to life style measurement: the universality of aspirations
3. Changing the price-performance envelope
4. Shift from low tech solution to universal access to high technology solutions
5. Provisioning of products and jobs for ecological vitality
6. Focus on governance

Essentially, these questions taken together force a new model for the economic development of a large, complex and highly pluralistic country like India. This model of development is best described as the Next Practice as this has not been tried anywhere else before on such a large scale. That should inspire us not to look outside for models (benchmarking best practices) but to look inside India and draw deeply on Her genius (as we did in the freedom movement). We need to invent the Next Practice of economic development. I will examine, below, each one of these mega-trends that provide the context for India's next phase of development.

1. *Shift from Abject Poverty to Income Inequality:*

India has reduced abject poverty dramatically during the last decade. However, there are a still 380.6 million[3] people in India who live on less than $ 1/day. It is safe to assume that "abject poverty" defined as living a "subsistence" existence on less than $ 1/day would be further reduced during the next 15 years. Abject poverty may not be the dominant concern in India@75. However, a more difficult problem will emerge in its place. An important consequence of rapid economic development and globalization of the economy are *the lags and asymmetries in the benefits that results*. Some sections of society will benefit (as those working in the IT industry) and some (illiterate labour in rural India) will lag behind. These asymmetries will create multiple, new divides in society – divides between educated and the uneducated, the urban and rural populations, between regions of the country as well as between ethnic groups. As a consequence, income inequality will emerge as a source of social tensions. This is not a uniquely Indian phenomenon. I must add that it is true of many rapidly growing economies such as China, Brazil, and S. Africa. It is also true of large economies undergoing rapid structural adjustment as in the USA. The Table 1 below illustrates the growing inequality as measured by Gini Coefficient.

Measures of Inequality:
Gini coefficient

	USA	China	India	Brazil	S Africa
1985-1986	41.6	22.4	32.0	59.3	
1989-1991	42.7	34.1	32.1	64.0	
1995-1996	45.0	39.0	33.8	60.2	
1999-2001	46.3	42.0	36.0	59.6	
2006	46.9	47.0	39.5	57.2	
GNI/capita PPP	$43,555	7,600	3,800	8,600	13,000
200 Rank in HD Index (177)	8	81	126	69	121

We can see that income inequality seems to result from rapid economic development and basic structural changes in an economy. The USA is not immune from this either. If we only considered one measure of inequality, income, then India does not look so bad. But consider two other measures; Income/per capita (measured in Purchasing Power Parity (PPP) (to reflect true local buying power) and the Human Development Index which is a measure of the inequalities of opportunities. On both these dimensions, India is at the low end. It is, therefore, not surprising that the masses in India are restless. India has to deal with a potent mix.

a. Low per capita income

b. A poor record of developing its human potential –education, and health, that lead to better opportunities

c. An environment that is creating asymmetric benefits (income inequalities).

d. India has a very young population. More than 52.3 %[4] of people are below the age of 25. As of 2025, we will still be a country of young people. 41.8 % of India will be less than 25 by 2025.

India has to reflect on how do we deal with this *combination of issues.* Should India focus on removing abject poverty by *increasing income* and create opportunity for people to move up the economic hierarchy - *income mobility* - and *provide hope?* Or should public policy be focused on reducing *income inequality?* The first order of business, I believe, is to be clear about the *distinctions between poverty (income level), lack of opportunity (income mobility) and income inequality.* Public debate in India does not make these distinctions. As a result, our prescriptions are not sharply focused on the problems that we need to solve. My preference is for creating income mobility more rapidly than we have done so far. This calls for a deep commitment to education and skill building. This also means not just growth (10% plus) but creating jobs fast (10 Million plus/year for the foreseeable future)[5]. Income mobility can be an effective antidote to social tensions arising from income inequality. The answer is not in going back to traditional approaches to reducing income inequality through taxing the rich and subsidizing the poor. We don't want to go back to the communist and the socialist dogma of keeping everybody poor so we have income equality. *We want rapid economic growth with high income mobility and lower income inequality.*

This debate gets played out in different ways. For example, I get asked very often whether globalization is good or bad for the poor. I say that is a wrong question. The question that we need to ask is how to *make globalization work for all. How we ask the question is extremely important on how we find the answer.* Globalization is like gravity. There is no point in *denying* gravity. We should *defy* gravity and build an airplane. *Inclusive growth is not about subsidies. It is about creating sustainable opportunities*. Both India and China are experiencing rapid growth, and both are struggling to find solutions to inclusive growth (India) and a harmonious society (China). India must innovate in this area.

2. *Shift from Income Levels to Lifestyle: Universality of Aspirations:*

While a discussion of per capita income dominates development literature and thinking, it sheds little light on how people live and what they hope for. The human dimension of poverty - aspirations of people takes a back seat. Consider for example, a life on $ 2/day. No person lives by herself or himself. People live in families. If we consider a family of five, the $2/day becomes $10/day and $3,650 per family per year. That is ₹146,000 per year for that family. We must recognize that the significant contributors to the consumer led growth in India are those who live on $2/day. The growth in two wheelers, cell phones, personal care products, textiles, private sector healthcare and education owe a lot to these families. We need in India to focus on the appropriate metrics to measure income mobility and inequality. Is it income or life style? For example, if we walk around in Dharavi, a slum in Mumbai, we are likely to find that people inside the hut may have a colour television set. They may also have a cooker, a cell phone, an electric iron, a fan and maybe a small refrigerator. Their lifestyles are very different from what it appears on the surface. It is a slum with no access to modern sewage, drinking water, or toilets. What do lifestyle measures mean and why we have to be focussed on it? 30-35% of India will live in slums in the next 20 years. We can designate them as *dense population clusters*. India needs to reflect on the implications of rapid urbanization even second and third tier cities. Do these developments provide new opportunities to solve the core societal problems or do they aggravate it?

When people come to the cities, whether small cities or big cities, their aspirations change dramatically. They look at the rich as a benchmark. They are exposed to more lifestyle information on bill boards, television and other media. Their income may not change as a rapidly as their aspirations change. Therefore, it is the lag between increasing aspirations and incomes that can fulfil those aspirations can lead to a significant increase in social unrest. I suggest a focus on *Lifestyle inequality*, the primary source of social tensions. If we conceptualize the problem as not just income inequality, but lifestyle inequalities, then we may have a solution to the problem.

3.   *Changing the Price-performance envelope*:

The combination of problems - low incomes, high aspirations and income inequalities may give one a moment of despair. How can we cope with these massive problems simultaneously? I believe that it is possible. We must focus on a fundamental change in the price performance levels of all products and services. The organized sector -- private and public -- primarily developed products and services for the rich and the well to do. The poor, the bottom of the pyramid consumers and producers, were below the radar screen of most organized sector. Therefore, we have had a situation where if we drew the price performance (value) envelope of products and services, it looks like the picture below (left).

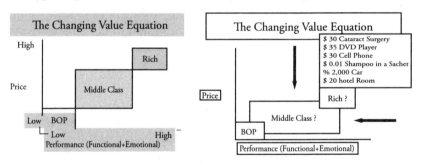

Traditionally, the poor, the middle class and the rich were seen as distinct segments. Products and services were developed with different performance characteristics. The functional, emotional and aesthetic aspects of performance differed. Price was based on the level of performance. Detergent which irritated your skin was acceptable for the poor. Cooking with biomass – a regressive fuel -- was acceptable. There was no need for LPG for the rural poor. There was an invisible but distinct "price-performance" (value) correlation as we moved from the poor to the rich segments. The emergence of the poor as consumers has altered this picture dramatically. Affordability to the new consumer, without a sacrifice in functional and emotional quality has changed the value equation. The $30 cataract surgery, $30 cell phone, $0.01 sachet of shampoo, $2,500 car, $100 computer, $25 hotel room are all illustrations of the dramatically changing value equation. This process is going to be accelerated. This increasing capacity to create life style equality can provide an antidote to increasing income inequality. This trend is likely to be further supported by the changing nature of high technology markets around the world.

4.   *Shift from Low Tech Solution to Universal Access to High Technology Solutions:*

Let us consider the dramatic changes in performance improvements in high technology components, as shown below in table 3:

Price-Performance Envelops are Changing Faster then anyone Expected

	1970	80	90	2006
1. Transistor/chip	10^3	-	10^6	10^9
2. Decrease in size of micro-device	-	10^{-1}	-	10^{-6}
3. Computer power	-	-	10^{11}	10^{15}
4. Cost per MIPs ($1000)	-	-	1	1M
5. DNA sequencing cost ($/BASE PAIR)	-	-	10	0.05
6. Magnetic data storage (bits/dollar)	10^4	-	-	10^{11}

Source: Ray Kurzwell

The rate at which the cost/unit of functionality is changing in high technology implies that the poor can afford products and services incorporating the latest technology - be it a cell phone or an iPod in a very short period of time. Further, many new sources of wealth such as access to information is becoming free as in the case of Google. Therefore, the pressure on price performance in emerging markets such as India can create a global phenomenon – dramatic decreases in prices and a fundamental realignment of cost structures. This process is already well underway as the examples from various industries demonstrate.

At these rates there is absolutely no reason why India cannot provide *the latest technology solutions* for everyone. That is good news. More people can afford things. More can fulfil their aspirations to a life style. The consequence of this rise in affordability is that it is going to create explosive growth in consumption. This huge market opportunity will also have significant implications to the environment and the demands it will put on it.

5.   *Provisioning of products and jobs for ecological vitality:*

What would happen if 800 million Indians become micro-consumers and micro-producers? The environmental impacts can be very significant. Whether it is water, energy, wastage and packaging, or the use of land, all ecosystems will be stressed. Sustainability is multidimensional. It is not just energy or water. It is not just waste. Unfortunately, ecological stresses hurt the poor first be it the cost of trucked in water or respiratory ailments due to the use biomass in cooking or stomach disorders due to unsafe drinking water.

The impact of rapid growth – consumption and production -- on ecosystems around the world, just not in India is critical for us to understand[6]. Ecological damage does not respect borders. We can consider the role of ecosystems as two fold – provision of food and water. Call it provisioning. Secondly, how do we regulate and protect these natural capital or natural resources? We can for example, protect ourselves against natural disasters such as floods. We could, for example, improve the sewage system in Mumbai and ensure that it can handle heavy rains during the monsoon. We can better regulate the spread of diseases such as malaria. We can control deforestation. Finally, we can enjoy the fruits of nature -- beautiful lakes, snow clad mountain peaks, and the sea. Nature can add to the quality of life. Worldwide, human ingenuity has found ways of improving nature's bounty. We grow more food per acre of land. We can say that provisioning is somewhat enhanced. However, regulation of natural capital provides a very mixed picture. Floods, drought, deforestation, and degradation of quality of land and water are well known. India needs to rapidly come to terms with it. I can share with you maps and satellite images that illustrate what is happening to the natural capital of India due to poor regulation and enforcement. Of the many areas that need immediate attention, I pick four:

1) the quality of water, its availability and access, the usage mix between   agriculture, industry and family use
2) energy
3) deforestation and
4) health. Health is closely associated with water and energy.

Poverty alleviation is not possible without thinking about sustainable development and the two are intimately linked. The current development models for energy, water, packaging, waste per capita are inappropriate and we have to develop fundamentally new ideas. India represents an ecological "time bomb". The shortage of water in urban India is already a major problem and it is likely to get worse. The cost of energy is already very high. These patterns of resource use are unsustainable. We have to find better use of resources and support new innovations in this area; better systems for cooking, better pricing and allocation of water for industrial, agricultural and domestic use, or better systems for waste reduction; including biodegradable packaging. I believe that affordable price performance levels, so critical for creating a fair and inclusive society will come with an ecological price tag. What are the preconditions for creating this kind of uninterrupted inclusive growth with ecological sensitivity?

6.   *Focus on Governance:*

Let us consider the relationship between GNI per capita in purchasing power terms, a country's score on the human development index and the quality of governance – i.e., the level of corruption. This information is publicly available for all countries. For example;

a. GNI/Capita in PPP terms is available from the World Bank
b. Human Development Index is available from UNDP
c. Corruption Index is available from Transparency International

If we use this data and look at both rich and poor countries we get very interesting correlations.

a. An analysis of Human Development Index and the Corruption

Perception Index, suggests that corrupt countries have lower level of human development.

b. If you look at the Corruption Perception Index and GDP/capita
in PPP terms, corrupt countries are not rich. Small subsets of the
populace in corrupt countries may be rich, but the country as a
whole is not rich.

c. If you look at Human Development Index and GDP/capita it is
the same pattern. The more you invest in your human resources
the richer the country gets.

These correlations are shown below. We can draw some important
conclusions from these correlations. In India, one can safely say that
the poor quality of human development is not about lack of resources.
It is about the level of corruption in the deployment of resources. Good
governance or less corruption leads to high levels of GDP per capita,
not the other way around. A nation does not get rich first and then become less corrupt. *A nation becomes less corrupt before it gets rich.* A focus
on human development is quite critical for getting rich. None of these
conclusions should come as a surprise. It is intuitively obvious but we
can look at the data from around the world and our conclusions are
further reinforced. I looked at India's GDP per capita in 2006 and the
rank in human development index (which is 126 out of 177). Nothing
much to be pleased about. Our corruption perception index was 3.3
(a very low grade out of ten, with very few countries being worse). We
have the opportunity to make significant improvements in these scores
by 2020 - both levels of corruption and Human Development Index.
India may not reach the level of Finland by that time, but even if we
reach a 7 on corruption (somewhere near the USA) and a rank of 20
out of 175 in human development Index, our per capita incomes will
move up dramatically – to say $25,000 PPP from the current level of
$3,800 PPP. The GDP gap this represents in total represents $28.2 tril-
lion. The explicit, quantifiable price we are paying for corruption and
the neglect of human resources in the country is staggering and should
be the focus of national debate.

Human Development Index (HDI) vs. Corruption Perception Index (CPI)

Corruption Perception Index (CPI) vs. Purchasing Power Parity (PPP)

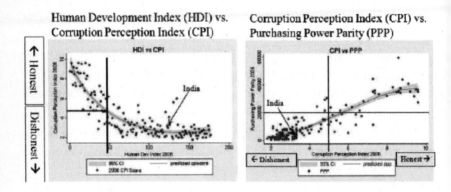

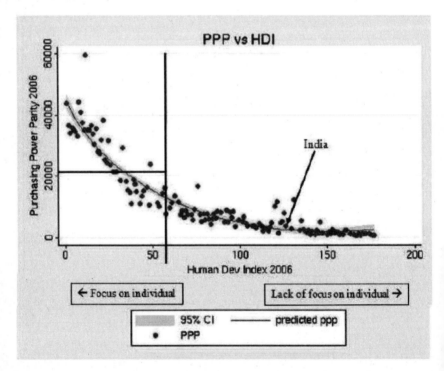

The trajectory we need to be on for dealing with corruption and with Human Development Index is not about more laws. I believe that we need to focus on a few basic areas.

    a. *Mental Models.* We need a serious examination of the mental models we use to think of India, its future, its developmental needs and the rights of individuals. What does it mean to be an Indian? What rights does citizenship bestow up on an individual citizen of India?

b. *Rights of Individuals vs. the Rights of Groups.* Closely associated with the rights of being an Indian is the focus on individual's rights. Indian politics is based on the rights of groups. We need a re-examination of the basic premise of "rights". Should the focus shift to the rights of the individual?

c. *Data Driven Solutions vs. Dogma Driven Solutions.* There is a lot of data that is available on every issue we have identified as critical so far. However, the debate is often ideological. Data gets distorted or worse not even used. History is full of examples of the human consequence of placing ideology over data driven reality. These include the millions who died in the gulags of Stalin or the famines of Mao. Democracy does not necessarily buffer a nation from the unintended negative consequences of poorly informed choices.

d. *Principles vs. Rituals.* We need to go back to the basic principles as the "tie breakers" when confronted with difficult decisions.

e. *Social Justice is not Socialism*: We should not confuse social justice, creating equal opportunities for all and eliminating inequalities with socialism. Socialism is an ideology and it has not succeeded anywhere in creating social equity with wealth creation.

f. *Accountability for Performance.* We need a better system for accountability. Infant mortality is about 2 million children per year due to infectious and diarrheal disease. Who is accountable for these "needless and preventable deaths"?

g. *Corruption as Treason.* Unless corruption at all levels is dealt with the seriousness of treason, it will be a very slow process of change.

h. *Focus on Imagination vs. a Focus on Resources.* How we deploy our resources to high impact opportunities may be more important than the sheer size of the resource base.

I recognize that these principles need a deep change in the culture of governance in India and a significant introspection. But I believe that this is crucial for transformative change in India.

The Innovation Sand Box

I have identified the key drivers of the developmental context for India@75. They relate not to abject poverty but income inequality, recognizing life styles, urbanization and the emergence of universal aspirations, a dramatic change in price-performance relationships, economic development and ecological crisis and finally the role of governance and the rule of law. Implicit in my discussion but crucial to understanding the process is the concept of scale. A country of the size of India – 1.2 billion people demands scale of operations that we have not even imagined thus far. Similarly, I have clearly focused on market based solutions. Both scale and market based approaches are implicit in this analysis.

The six issues that I identified as providing the context for India@75 cannot be ignored. All development must embrace these constraints and treat them as "non-negotiables". We have to innovate within these constraints. To demonstrate the criticality of these constraints, I developed the notion of an *innovation sand box or a development sandbox*. The social

The "Sandbox" for Economic Development

Global Scale

Rule of Low, Individual Rights

Environmentally Sustainable

Innovation within These Constraints

Social Equity Focus

New Price-Performance Levels

Market Based

equity focus recognizes the need for income equality, the Rule of law constraint refers to key governance issues raised earlier, the environmentally sustainable constraint refers to the need of ecological vitality and the new price-performance constraints clearly incorporates the changing price performance envelope we discussed earlier. We know we can operate within these constraints and innovate. For example, we are cracking the price-performance envelope successfully. We are scaling rapidly. The value of market based systems is gaining momentum. We are getting some understanding of the ecological needs whether in the use of CNG in transportation or rain water harvesting. We have made very little progress in imposing the rule of law, in improving governance or in dealing with social equity through market based mechanisms. The sandbox represented below puts all these requirements together and suggests that all innovations, policy decisions, and priorities must be done within this sandbox. I say don't violate these constraints. Work within these constraints. As long as we innovate within those constraints we will do exceptionally well. It must be the same sandbox for politicians, bureaucrats, business men, NGOs and private citizens. While the approach to innovations can vary, the boundary conditions must be the same.

The potential of India@75 that I presented at the beginning of this lecture is possible if we are disciplined in accepting the constraints and executing within the sandbox. I have been always optimistic about India's future. I thought I would finish by going back to a presentation I made in 1989 at a CII Conference. My view of India, as I saw its future in 1989 is shown here:

If we looked the industrial landscape

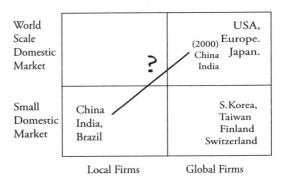

The Emerging World Order: My View in 1989

of the world at that time, there were global firms and local firms. Some countries represented a large (world scale) domestic market and some small domestic markets. Global firms emanated from countries with small domestic markets such as Finland, The Netherlands and Switzerland as well as from the USA, Japan and Germany. However, there were few countries which could claim, that they are home to global firms as well as represent world scale domestic markets. India at that time had no global firm and had a very small domestic market. My prediction was that by 2000, India and China will join the select group of counties such as USA, Germany and Japan. We are not there yet but we are well on the way. The G-7 and G-8 may have to formally include India in the future. At that time there were not too many believers. Now it is becoming a reality. All of us here believe that India has earned her place in the world economic order.

I think the poor in India are ready for the journey. I think the problem is with the elites of India and with India's political leaders across the spectrum. I believe that if you want to understand India we have to go back to her deep past. The recent past does not give us many clues to Her genius. The first ethicist in India and maybe the world was the Tamil saint Thiruvalluvar. He said something dramatic: *"Even if God wills against you, hard work will get you there"*. 2000 years ago, he told us: "don't blame anybody else except yourself." I believe there is nothing more powerful than Indians taking responsibility for their own future. If India@75 fails to become a global leader the only reason for that failure will be Indians themselves. Nobody from outside is stopping us from succeeding. So this transformation is not about resources. It is about our confidence in building a new India. If we cannot imagine this India we cannot create it. Imagination and belief in India's true destiny is what we need. We need the passion, the courage and certainly an enormous dose of humanity and humility.

Thank you.

References

[1] *The Knowledge Commission* under the leadership of Mr. Sam Pitroda and the *Skills Commission* under the leadership of ......are good starts in this direction.

[2] C.K. Prahalad: The Fortune at the Bottom of the Pyramid: Eradicating Poverty through Profits, Wharton Publishing, 2004 and C.K. Prahalad: the Innovation Sand box; Strategy+ Business, 2007

[3] World Resources Institute

[4] Source: UN Population division: World Population Prospects 2006

[5] I have talked about 10% growth and 10 million new jobs for several years starting 2002.

[6] World Resources Institute

Acknowledgements

Divine interventions come in strange ways. If a large-hearted schizo-phrenic man had not hallucinated about funding ManagementNext magazine, and not asked me to meet him, I wouldn't have gone to Chennai on August 7, 2011, the same day the first *CK Prahalad Memorial Lecture* was organized by Loyola Institute of Business Administration (LIBA). I had requested the event organizer to courier the DVD.

Listening to the top CEOs at the memorial on how they were chastised, verbally spanked and then mentored and coached by CK, the book idea was born right there. When Westland said yes to my book proposal, all in a week, and that too with a small advance, the book was on. Thanks to Karthik Venkatesh, who is also the Editor of this book, and to Paul Vinay Kumar, the Publisher, for their confidence in me.

The fascinating chapter 'Man Behind the Guru' which takes a peek into the early life of CK and his influences, would not have been possible without the whole-hearted support of CK's family, his wife Mrs. Gayatri Prahalad and his two children Deepa and Murali. Special thanks to Deepa for being the patient link with the family.

This book would not have happened if India's top business leaders had not believed in the idea of this book. Special thanks to Ratan Tata, Adi Godrej, Anand Mahindra, Arun Maira, Tarun Das, Krishna Kumar, B Muthuraman, S Ramadorai, Jay Varadaraj, Ashok Soota, Sridhar Mitta, MR Rangaswami, Stuart Hart, Som Mittal, Ravi Venkatesan, Prof. Sadagopan, GV Sanjay Reddy, Jamshyd Godrej and Jerry Rao for their time and for sharing their inspired experience.

Although the book's focus is to tell the untold story of the profound impact CK made on the minds and dreams of a good number of Indian business leaders since the 1991 reforms, I felt readers would expect to read about CK's big impact on management ideas and thinking through books and articles. I'm grateful to Prof. S Manikutty for the chapter on distilling CK's work.

In true CK's style of co-creation, I reached out to Subroto Bagchi, MR Rangaswami, Rama Bijapurkar, Stuart Hart and Shankar P for their critical comments on some chapters and the book title. It's an interesting coincidence that it was Shankar P, as my boss in *The Economic Times*, who had asked me to interview CK in 1996.

I've dedicated this book to The Jesuit Fathers because they have been my strongest support, especially Fr. Claude D'Souza, who first gave me the opportunity to travel and write about the social and economic challenges faced by the disadvantaged, in several districts of Karnataka, while I was still in the university. It's a happy coincidence that CK did his graduation in a Jesuit institution, Loyola College, Chennai, and he got his first break in corporate life because his principal recommended him.

However profound an idea, there's a lot of work that goes into producing a book. Suchitra Jayaprabhu's painstaking transcriptions and co-coordinating interviews were a big help.

My gratitude to my father, Joseph Bobby, who made me believe in the power of audacious goals; to my father-in-law Rajshekhar Mansur and wife Sangeeta Mansur for their support.